bright & breezy
patchwork

Over 30 fresh quilting and patchwork projects

 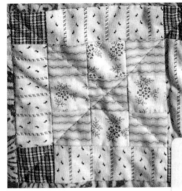 

R. Norum & H.A. Krohg

D&C

David and Charles

A DAVID & CHARLES BOOK

Copyright © J.W. Cappelens Forlag AS 2007
www.cappelen.no
Originally published in Norway as *Quiltegleder*

First published in the UK in 2008 by David & Charles
David & Charles is an F+W Publications Inc. company
4700 East Galbraith Road
Cincinnati, OH 45236

A catalogue record for this book is available from the British Library.

ISBN-13: 978-0-7153-2917-7 paperback
ISBN-10: 0-7153-2917-0 paperback

Printed in China by RR Donnelley
for David & Charles
Brunel House   Newton Abbot   Devon

Visit our website at www.davidandcharles.co.uk

David & Charles books are available from all good bookshops; alternatively you can
contact our Orderline on 0870 9908222 or write to us at FREEPOST EX2 110, D&C
Direct, Newton Abbot, TQ12 4ZZ (no stamp required UK only); US customers call
800-289-0963 and Canadian customers call 800-840-5220.

Contents

3   Introduction
4   Materials
5   Equipment
7   Techniques
16 Factors for success
18 Composing a quilt

20 Dear Maggie
24 Edouard
26 Gorgeous Grey
30 Summer Memories
32 Midsummer Flower Garland
36 Golden Days
38 Red, White and Blue
40 A Cup of Tea
44 Diamonds are Forever
46 Lucky Retro
50 Puss in the Corner
52 It Takes Two
56 Stargazer
58 Star Boat
62 Star Boat Tablecloth
64 All in a Row
66 Buttoned up Bag
70 Just Like Old Times
74 Princesses Have Fun
76 Sitting Pretty
80 Sweet Dreams
84 For a Little Gentleman
86 A Page to Colour…
90 Ric's Rag Rug
92 Green Tweed Handbag
94 Brown Tweed Bag
96 Dear Hattie
98 Dressed for the Party
100 Flowers for Abelone
104 Wheels on the Bus

107 Stockists
108 Patterns
120 Postscript

Introduction

The designs in this book have been sewn by Rie Norum and Hilde Aanerud Krohg. We are both 'thirty-something' and between us we have four children between the ages of one and seven. We are both electrical engineers and when we first met on a weekend course arranged by a patchwork club near Oslo, we quickly hit it off. We've always got plenty to talk about and lots of projects waiting to be sewn. Patchworking brings us a lot of pleasure and we think it is the best hobby in the world.

We are always on the look-out for new fabrics – in patchwork shops, flea markets, interior decorating shops, Mum's needlework chest and among Grandma's cast-off bed-linen. We often help ourselves from each other's piles of fabrics. It is easily as much fun as trading stickers!

There is so much room for variation and so many techniques that we never stop learning something new, and are never bored. In this book we present a new technique for sewing perfectly round circles using a sewing machine – without pins. Great fun!

Probably one of the best things about patchworking is that most errors can be corrected; it is rarely necessary to unpick seams. You can sew a button over a crooked corner or appliqué a heart over a hole or a blemish in your fabric.

In a number of the patterns in this book we refer to paintings and other sources of inspiration. There are so many beautiful things around us which can provide inspiration when we are sewing quilts. We recommend you to keep your eyes open and make notes as you go along. Tiled floors can contain fine geometrical shapes which are suitable for patchwork; make a sketch of them, or take a photo with your mobile phone. In time you will be seeing patchwork quilts everywhere! We cut out and collect attractive pictures and seek out fabrics with suitable colours, patterns and moods.

The book describes many quilts and bags of varying degrees of difficulty. If we have inspired you to give it a try, start by sewing some blocks and improvize as you go along – you can add or remove blocks from a piece or add an extra border. Some or all of the colours can be replaced, so that you get a quilt which appeals to your own taste and colour preferences, and which becomes your own design! In any event it is a good idea to read through the whole pattern before you start sewing. That way you will see it as a whole and understand all the explanations.

Best wishes

Rie and Hilde

Materials

Fabrics

Most of the quilts in this book have been made using 100 per cent cotton fabric which is particularly suitable for quilting. In many of the designs each fabric has been used just once, resulting in wide variation in colours, patterning and shades. The choice of fabric depends entirely on what sort of mood or atmosphere you wish your quilt to conjure up. In the past, people used what fabrics they had to hand, and the result could be unexpected and interesting. We have tried to carry on this tradition of using unusual and unexpected colour and pattern combinations. We have selected a wide range of fabrics from old reproductions and shirting fabrics to the more modern fabrics designed by Rowan and Amy Butler. The shirting fabrics resemble old-fashioned shirt fabrics and the reproductions are reprints of old fabric patterns from up to several hundred years ago. The Japanese fabrics which have become available on the market in recent years are beautiful and popular. They have a slightly muted character and often subdued patterns. Linen and coarsely woven Japanese fabrics have also become popular and lend structure to surfaces. Some of the bag designs use denim fabric. Whichever fabrics you prefer to use in your projects, it is definitely an advantage to wash them first. This shrinks them and removes any surplus dye, and last but not least it removes the sizing which is used to treat woven fabrics to enhance their colours and keep their shape. Some people may have an allergic reactions to the sizing, such as nasal congestion, watering eyes, itching and rashes. Clearly, no quilter wants this to happen.

Pearls and sequins

Sew on pearls and sequins are available in many sizes, colours and materials. We have used small, translucent plastic sequins and some bronze-coloured metal ones. You can find both sequins and pearls in craft shops.

Ribbon

Another way to decorate quilts is to use ribbons. We have used cotton ribbon and sequined ribbon which is bought by length. Cotton ribbons should be shrunk before they are sewn on, either by washing them or by steam ironing. This prevents them shrinking and creating wrinkles in your quilt after washing.

Buttons

Some of the designs have been decorated with buttons, and there are masses of these to choose from. We have used lots of mother-of-pearl buttons because of their attractive colours and lustre, but metal, glass and plastic buttons have also found their way into our work.

Quilt backing

When choosing quilt backing it is wise to use cotton fabrics and not the cheaper synthetics which can be difficult to quilt because they slip in the sewing machine. There are wide cotton fabrics available which are intended for use as backing for quilts. You can also make a quilt backing piece out of a number of scraps of fabric that you have in your box of oddments. The quilt backing needs to be two to four inches larger than the front on all four sides. If you choose a backing with a busy pattern it will be easier to conceal any unevenness in the quilting than it would be with a regular geometric pattern or plain fabric. Another way to make the quilting fit in well with the backing is to choose a backing fabric whose colour is the same as the thread you use for the quilting. This requires some planning, but the advantage is that you can use the same colour for the upper and shuttle threads in your machine.

Thread

To sew blocks together we use cotton thread in colours that match the fabrics. You could use a universal grey-beige colour which will match most fabrics.

The type of quilting thread used depends on whether you are quilting on a machine or by hand. There are various types on the market, from pure cotton threads to wool, linen and silk, as well as blends. We have used a lot of silk thread in our quilting, in colours which blend into the fabrics and provide an attractive shading effect.

For a decorative quilt, stitch on appliqué and for making tassels for tablecloths we have used DMC mouliné embroidery thread made from 100 per cent cotton.

Cotton thread is particularly suitable for tacking (basting) and it can be bought on large bobbins which last for a very long time. Water-soluble thread is also available, which does not have to be removed at all because it simply dissolves the first time that it is washed.

Batting

The type of batting you choose is down to personal taste and depends on whether you are quilting by hand or are using a machine, and whether you prefer a smooth or wrinkled appearance. Woollen batting is suitable for both hand and machine quilting. Passing a needle through it is like a hot knife going through butter and this makes it particularly good for hand quilting. Woollen batting is light, hardly shrinks at all and provides volume, often resembling trapunto quilting in which extra batting is stuffed into the work at the end to give a three-dimensional effect. Cotton batting is somewhat heavier but shrinks much more, often up to 3 per cent, resulting in quite an antique appearance. Thin cotton batting is suitable for both machine and hand quilting while the thickest ones are best for quilting with a machine. There is also a batting made from a blend of cotton and synthetic fibres. This is often referred to as 80/20, since it is composed of 80 per cent cotton and 20 per cent synthetic. These types of batting are suitable for both machine and hand quilting, and tend to be easier to hand quilt with than pure cotton batting. Totally synthetic batting is usually most suitable for machine quilting. It is available with or without an adhesive side. Synthetic batting does not shrink, giving your quilting projects an even appearance.

If you have any batting remnants left over it is wise to label them so that you know what they are made from later on. This is particularly important if you ever need to join pieces of batting together.

Equipment

Pencils and marking chalk

To draw patterns on freezer paper we use a 0.5mm clutch pencil with an HB lead. Fabric marking chalk or pencil is used to draw the quilting patterns. You can also use a clutch pencil with a 2B lead. The pencil lines will disappear during washing or can be removed using a special eraser.

Rulers

Rulers of various lengths are useful, since having a ruler of the same length as the block you are making saves time.

Compass

A compass was used to draw the circles in the patterns.

Tulle

This is a synthetic netting fabric which can be used to transfer quilting patterns to fabric. Draw the pattern on a piece of tulle using a waterproof felt pen. Place the tulle on your fabric and trace the pattern with a 2B pencil, letting the pencil point penetrate through the holes in the tulle. Remove the tulle and you are ready to start quilting.

Freezer paper

Freezer paper has a matt and a glossy side. The glossy side is covered with a thin plastic coating which melts like wax when you iron it on to fabric. The paper has lots of uses and in quilting it is very suitable, among other things, for appliqué, reverse appliqué by hand and machine and for making parts of patterns. Draw the pattern on the matt side. Cut it out and place the glossy side against the fabric and iron on the matt side. The freezer paper will stick to the fabric but can be pulled off. The paper can be used repeatedly until it no longer adheres to the fabric when ironed.

Note: freezer paper may shrink when it is ironed, so it is wise to place it on a surface which it will not adhere to and steam iron it before drawing the quilt block pattern on it. This is particularly important when you draw large blocks as in the 'Star boat' quilt. Do not iron with steam later in the process as the paper may become firmly stuck to the fabric. Always test the iron to make sure

you are using the right temperature. If the iron is too warm, the paper may adhere too well to the fabric and be impossible to remove. In some cases ironing it again will allow you to lift it. If it is still impossible to remove, the solution is to wash the block after it has been sewn.

You can print a block or pattern directly from a computer on to freezer paper using an ink-jet printer. It is not possible to print on it using a laser printer.

Pattern paper

This paper is available with or without a printed grid in inches or centimetres. For large pattern elements, such as the 34in diameter circles for the bags on page 66, pattern paper can be a great help. Draw the pattern element on the paper, cut it out and pin it to the fabric, then cut out the piece of fabric.

Pattern adhesive

You can attach a pattern to your fabric using adhesive instead of pins. Spray pattern adhesive directly on to the pattern paper, which is then placed on the fabric. After you have cut out the pattern it can be pulled off the fabric and used again.

Spray adhesive

Temporary spray adhesive is a fast and easy way to hold quilt layers together. The adhesive is also suitable for appliqué work, reversed appliqué on a machine and for tacking (basting) quilts before you begin quilting. The adhesive is not permanent and disappears completely after a short time. If you use spray adhesive, it is wise to wash your work immediately after you have finished, so that you aren't breathing in fumes from the adhesive for a long period of time and to avoid any discolouration of the fabric.

Bias tape for appliqué

An apparatus for making bias tape is a great time-saver. We have used a fusible bias tape maker and fusible web. The former is an appliance which folds fabric strips into bias tape, while the latter is an interfacing tape on a roll which is threaded into the tape maker. When using it you can fold bias tape and add iron-on interfacing tape at the same time. Remove the paper from the interfacing tape and you are ready to iron the bias tape on to the fabric.

Quilt templates on a roll

Ready-made quilt borders can be bought in rolls of different widths. The paper border has adhesive tape along the edges so that it isn't necessary to fix it with pins. Follow the ready-drawn lines, sewing through both the paper and the quilt. Remove the paper when all the lines have been sewn. You can also buy quilt paper in rolls, with or without tape, and without ready-drawn patterns. Use it to transfer your own pattern on to fabric. If you use the type without tape edges pattern adhesive can be used to hold the pattern instead of pins. Greaseproof paper can also be used to transfer patterns, but it is slippery, difficult to sew on and more difficult to tear off than quilt paper in a roll. If you have chosen a border which is not of the required width, you can enlarge or reduce it using a photocopier before tracing it on to the paper.

Plastic quilting templates

Plastic templates have cut out slots to follow when drawing the pattern. The template is placed on the fabric and you mark the pattern through the slots. You can do this using a heramarker (a plastic knife which leaves a shiny line on the fabric), marking chalk or a 2B pencil. The template has a single pattern repeat which is moved along the border. If you want to make your own plastic templates, you can buy the plastic sheet and a special cutting knife with a double blade to cut the slots in the plastic.

Protective spray

A protective spray can be bought which protects quilts against dust, dirt and ultra-violet radiation.

Adhesive pattern paper

The adhesive is on one side only and it is often used for appliqué such as the cups on the 'Cup of Tea' quilt.

Interfacing

Made of synthetic fibre, interfacing is sold in different weights and can have adhesive on one or both sides. It is used to reinforce or stiffen fabrics. Iron it with the adhesive side against the wrong side of the fabric. Double sided interfacing has a protective sheet which is removed before ironing.

Fabric interfacing

This woven or knitted material is often a blend of natural and synthetic fibres. It may be with or without an adhesive side. For designs like the handbag and pouffes in this book, fabric interfacing with an adhesive side was used to reinforce thin cotton fabrics. Iron it with the adhesive side against the wrong side of the fabric.

Paper templates

Paper templates that are used for English patchwork can be bought ready-made or you can make them yourself. Plastic stencils or templates are available in a variety of patchwork shapes. Draw round them on ordinary paper or thin card and cut them out using paper scissors.

Techniques

Thread tension

Some sewing machines adjust the thread tension automatically according to the type of fabric and seam selected, others have to be adjusted manually. When adjusting the thread tension you should test it by sewing zigzag stitches. If the tension is too loose the shuttle thread will be straight and the upper thread will be pulled down to the underside. If the tension is too tight the upper thread will be straight and the shuttle thread will be pulled up to the surface of the fabric. When the tension is correct, the threads will engage each other midway between the fabric layers.

Assembly

When sewing blocks together, use straight stitches with a length of $^{1}/_{16}$in. This way, you will not need to fix the thread at the start and finish of a seam. If your machine has a tendency to pull the fabric down through the stitch plate at the beginning of a seam, use a small piece of fabric to sew over before continuing on to the work. This is almost like chain sewing.

Chain sewing

When sewing several pieces of fabric together chain sewing them can save thread and time as you don't need to cut the thread for each piece. This also reduces the risk of the machine pulling at the fabric at the start of each seam. When you reach the end of the first piece, place the next under the pressure foot, sewing continuously instead of stopping and cutting the thread. When the first piece has emerged from under the pressure foot it can be cut off, or you can continue sewing and do the cutting later.

Ironing

Get to know your iron! It is constantly in use in quilting to produce good results. Iron on the wrong side whenever possible and avoid using steam as this can cause the fabric to be pulled out of shape. If you haven't washed the fabrics beforehand, they may shrink when exposed to steam, and the resulting block will be too small. When sewing quilt blocks you should iron the seam allowance against the darkest fabric. However, there is an exception to every rule and the important thing is to plan which way the seam allowance is to be laid beforehand. If you are sewing together blocks and sashings and want all the seam allowances to fold towards or away from the blocks, you must bear this in mind and plan your ironing. The same applies when sewing together rows of squares. The allowances are ironed in alternating directions, regardless of the colours of the fabrics, as described under Nine-patch blocks on page 8.

Four-patch blocks

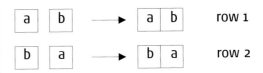

A four-patch block is made up of four squares. Sew together the squares in pairs.

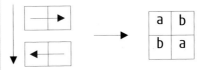

The seams should be ironed in opposite directions in rows 1 and 2, as indicated by the red arrows. Sew the two rows together to form a four-patch block. Make sure that the seams meet exactly at the centre of the block.

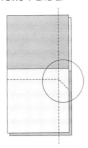

When you have sewn together the two rows, remove the stitches in the seam allowance which you made when sewing together rows 1 and 2.

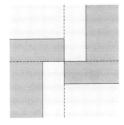

Use your fingers to twist the seam allowances around the centre of the block.

Press down the seams and the result is a nice, flat block without a lump in the middle.

Nine-patch blocks

A nine-patch block is made up of nine squares.
Sew the squares together in three rows of three.

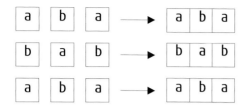

The seams should be ironed in alternate directions in rows 1, 2 and 3, as for the four-patch block. Sew the three rows together to form a nine-patch block. Make sure that the seams meet exactly at the centre of the block.

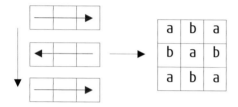

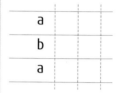

Iron the seam allowance against the darkest material if you prefer to divide the seam allowances in the same way as in the four-patch blocks.

Strip set for four-patch blocks

This is a time-saving technique when you want to sew a large number of four-patch blocks.

Sew together one (a) strip (width of square × whole width of the fabric) and one (b) strip (width of square × whole width of fabric) to make a strip set. Cut vertical strips, the same width as the square, from the strip set. Iron the seam allowance against the darkest fabric. You need twice as many strips as the number of blocks you want to sew.

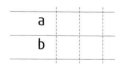

Sew together strip sets in pairs to form a four-patch block.

a	b
b	a

Flip the seam allowance at the joins in the same way as described on page 7 for the four-patch blocks.

Strip set for nine-patch blocks

Making strip sets is also a time-saving technique when you want to sew a large number of nine-patch blocks.

Sew together one (a) strip (width of square × whole width of the fabric) and two (b) strips (width of square × whole width of fabric) to make a strip set. Cut strips, the same width as the square, vertically from the strip set. Always iron seam allowances against the darkest fabric.

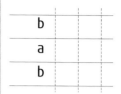

Sew together one (b) strip (width of square × whole width of the fabric) and two (a) strips (width of square × whole width of fabric) to make a strip set. Cut vertical strips the same width as the square from the strip set. You need twice as many strips as in Step 1. Iron the seam allowance against the darkest fabric.

Sew together one (bab) strip set and two (aba) strip sets.

a	b	a
b	a	b
a	b	a

Flip the seam allowance at the joins in the same way as for the four-patch block.

Quick corners

This is a good technique for sewing corner triangles to a square. Place a corner square on the larger square, right sides facing and raw edges matching. Mark the seam diagonally on the corner square and sew along the line. Cut off the corner, leaving a ¼ in seam allowance. Fold the corner back and press the seam allowance against the darker fabric.

The corner piece can be a square, rectangle or any other shape, as long as it has a 90 degree corner.

English patchwork

This old technique involves hand sewing around paper templates. It is simple to do and can be used to sew intricate patterns while getting all the corners and points to meet each other. You can work in suitably sized units and a small unit can be carried in a handbag to sew when one has a few minutes to spare.

Cut the patchwork pieces out of paper if you don't have ready-made templates. Pin the template to the fabric and cut out with a seam allowance ¼in wider than the template on all sides. Fold in the seam allowance, making sure that the edges are straight and sharp. Tack (baste) the corners together as you move around the paper template. If you are making diamonds make sure you fold all the points in the same direction so that they twist themselves nicely around the mid-point without making a lump. With large paper templates, such as 3in diamonds, it may be necessary to baste through the paper along the edges. With smaller paper templates you only need to baste through the fabric, and then you won't need to remove the tacking stitches. If you baste through the paper, make sure the knot on the thread where you start the seam is on the right side of the fabric. This makes it easier to see and to pull out when the stitches are to be removed. If you prefer you can tape the seam allowances together with masking tape.

When sewing the pieces together, place them with right sides facing and sew with small neat stitches along the edges. Fix the thread well at the start and finish of each seam. The paper template is removed when each piece has been sewn to all the surrounding parts.

Diamonds

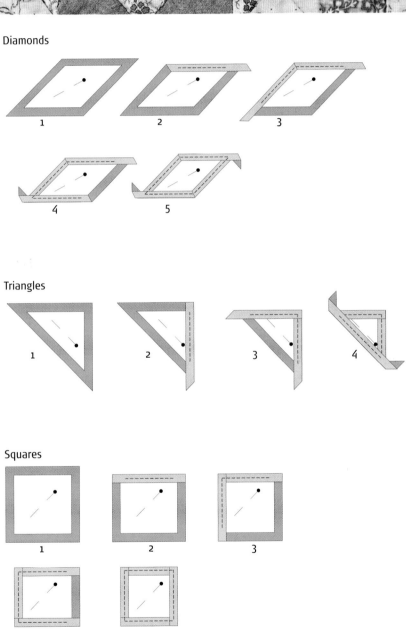

Triangles

Squares

Appliqué using freezer paper

Iron the freezer paper on to the fabric. Cut out leaving a seam allowance of about ¼in from the edge of the paper. Tack (baste) around the seam allowance and pull tight so that the fabric folds in over the paper. Press the edge down, using your fingers or an iron, to make a nice, smooth curve and tie off the thread. Remove the freezer paper and the part is ready to be appliquéd in place.

viewed from the wrong side

An alternative to tacking (basting) is to cut notches all round the seam allowance, cover the freezer paper and spray with adhesive. Fold in the seam allowance, and iron. The allowance will rise when the adhesive dries so that you can remove the freezer paper. Fold the allowance down again and the part is ready to be appliquéd in place. Use pins, adhesive or tack (baste) the part in position before stitching it in place.

Reverse appliqué by hand

Using the reverse appliqué technique creates depth because the appliqué fabric is placed behind the backing fabric instead of on top of it as in ordinary appliqué.

Trace the appliqué shape on freezer paper (A). Remember to make a mirror-image of the block if it is not symmetrical both vertically and horizontally.

Cut out and iron the freezer paper on the wrong side of the backing fabric with the glossy side down (B). Make the straight edges of the paper lie along the weave of the fabric.

Cut out the opening in the backing fabric following the inner edge of the freezer paper and about ¼in from the line (C). This forms the seam allowance on the backing fabric. Cut slits across the seam allowance, about ¼in apart and no closer than 2-3 threads from the edge of the freezer paper.

Fold the seam allowance against the freezer paper and the wrong side of the backing fabric and tack (baste) in place (D). Lay the appliqué fabric behind the backing fabric (E) and pin or baste it in place. Sew along the edge of the backing fabric with invisible stitching, using thread of the same colour as the background fabric. Remove the basting stitches or pins and the freezer paper, and trim the seam allowance (G).

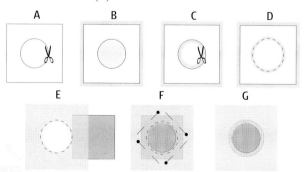

Reverse appliqué by machine

Reverse appliqué can also be sewn by machine instead of by hand. Follow Steps (A) to (C) as for reverse appliqué by hand. In Step (C) you must also draw a pencil line (as thinly and accurately as possible) on the fabric around the inner edge of the hole in the freezer paper.

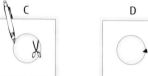 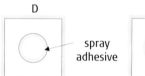

Spray adhesive along the cut edge (D), taking care to get the adhesive only on the fabric. To avoid spraying on the freezer paper, draw the block on ordinary paper, cut out the centre and fix the paper on the freezer paper covering it exactly while you spray the adhesive. Fold the fabric against the freezer paper on the wrong side of the fabric (E).

Apply adhesive using a glue stick along the edge of the fabric (F). Avoid getting glue on the freezer paper as this may be difficult to remove before the blocks are sewn together.

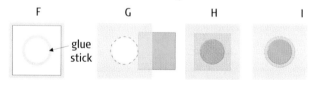

Place the fabric and freezer paper with its wrong side against the right side of the appliqué part (G). Using an iron on the wrong side, press lightly around the edge to fix the adhesive.

Let the adhesive dry completely before you remove the freezer paper, or it will stick to the pressure foot of your machine when you start sewing! Check with your finger; if still sticky, iron it some more.

Lay the block with its right side up and sew along the seam allowance on the backing fabric, along the marked line. Trim the seam allowance (I) and iron the block on the wrong side.

A final tip:

Because this technique uses spray adhesive and glue stick, it is a good idea to wash the finished quilt so that you aren't breathing in fumes from the glues and to avoid any discolouration of the fabric.

Piecing using freezer paper

You can only sew in straight lines using this technique. Draw the pattern on freezer paper, cut it out and fold along all the lines. The pattern shown here is one half of a pinwheel block.

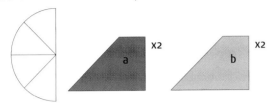

Iron the freezer paper, with the glossy side against the fabric, on to the wrong side of one of the triangles (a) or (b), as shown in the diagram below. Make sure you start with the same fabric in both halves if you are making two.

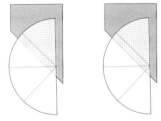

Fold the freezer paper back, place a new triangle with its right side against the first part and sew along the edge of the paper. Be careful not to sew through the paper! Fold the fabric against the freezer paper and iron flat.

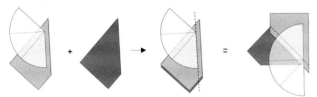

Continue until the semicircle is complete. To make a pinwheel, make two semicircles, pin them together and sew them together across the centre. The freezer paper is removed at the end and can be re-used many times.

Zip fasteners

Before you start, mark the points at which the zip fastener starts and finishes on the fabric. Pin the two pieces together and start to sew using a 1 in n seam allowance and stopping at the first mark for the zip. Increase the stitch length and continue sewing to the second mark. Reduce the stitch size and sew to the end. Iron the seam allowances open. Place the zip with its right side against the seam allowance and pin in place. Use a zip foot and large stitches to tack (baste) the zip to the seam allowance. With the fabric right side up, and the zip foot in the left-hand position so that the needle goes down on the left-hand side of the foot, place the foot to the right and at the bottom of the zip fastener. Sew across the bottom, turn the fabric and sew all the way along the right-hand side of the zip. Switch the zip foot to the right-hand position so that the needle goes down on the right-hand side of the foot. Place the foot to the left of the zip fastener, and sew all the way along the left-hand side of the zipper. Remove the large stitches between the marks.

Piping cords

Cut 1 in wide strips at 45 degrees to the weave of the fabric, making enough for the length of the piping cord, including joins. Join the strips by laying them right sides facing, and matching short ends, as shown in the diagram below. Sew a seam ¼ in from the edge and press the seams open. Trim off the 'ears' that stick out at the edges of the strip.

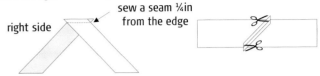

Lay the piping cord on the wrong side of the fabric strip and fold the strip over it. Make sure that the fabric edges meet and pin together (optional).

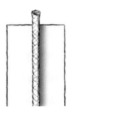

With the cord on the left and the raw edges to the right, sew a seam alongside the cord using a cord edge foot or zip foot. If you use a cord edge foot, place it with the cord in the slot in the foot and the needle in the centre position. If you use a zip foot, place it in the left-hand position with the needle in the left-hand position. Don't sew too close to the cord, as you are going to sew another two seams just inside this seam. If you sew this first seam too close to the cord it will be difficult to hide it using the next two seams.

Lay the finished piping on the right side of your fabric with the raw edges along the cut edges of the fabric. Sew to the fabric in the same way as when you made the piping, but this time sewing just inside the previous seam.

Now place the other piece of fabric with its right side facing the first fabric. The piping will now be between the two layers of fabric. With the first seam upwards, sew the layers together, stitching just inside the previous seam.

Unless you remove a little of the cord, a lump may form where the ends of the cord meet. Cut the ends of the piping so that they overlap by 1–1½ in as shown. Pull the cord 1–1½ in out of the fabric and cut diagonally inwards, being careful not to cut the fabric. Pull the cord back into the fabric again and join the ends by crossing them over and sewing them together. Trim the ends of the piping that stick out beyond the raw edge.

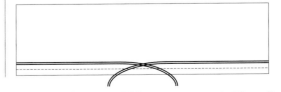

Joining batting

Sometimes you will need to join batting. Joins should never be completely straight, as this will result in a dent in your quilt, however thickly you quilt it. Instead, you should make a wavy join, as follows:

Place the pieces of batting that you want to join next to each other, with an overlap of 2–4in (see diagram): Use a cutting wheel to cut a wavy line through both layers of the batting. Carefully remove the surplus batting above and below, without moving the batting which is to be joined. Make a mark on each side so that you know where the pieces of batting are to meet when you sew them together. Place the batting pieces against each other and sew the edges together on a machine using a decorative stitch (1) or a zigzag tacking stitch (2).

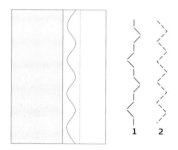

1   2

Basting

When the quilt front is finished, it is tacked (basted) to the batting and backing fabric. You can either sew by hand or use spray adhesive, a tacking (basting) gun or curved safety pins to hold the layers together while you quilt.

Personalizing your quilt

When we sew patchwork quilts, we are making heirlooms for coming generations. It isn't always easy to remember who made what and when, so you should always mark your quilts with important information, such as: Made by/ Date/ For whom/ On what occasion/ Name of pattern.

You can make your own labels or buy them ready-made, appliqué them on at the end or sew them into the backing fabric. If you have a patchwork block left over, you can use it as a label. You can also write the details with a felt pen or embroider them directly on to the quilt.

Quilting

The quilting technique is used to attach the layers of fabric and batting to each other. It can be done on a sewing machine or by hand, or by a combination of both. Use suitable thread in colours which match the quilt. The recommended distance between quilt seams can usually be found on the packet in which the batting is bought. If you use a greater distance, the batting may form lumps during washing. The thickness of the batting used will also have an effect on the appearance of the quilt pattern. A thick batting produces a more 'bubbly' look than a thin one with the same distance between the quilt seams. A thick batting should, therefore, be quilted with a more open pattern than a thin batting. If the quilting is too tightly spaced, the quilt can easily become flat and inflexible.

The choice of quilt pattern and thread is important to bring out the attractiveness of the quilt. If your quilt is to have several borders, don't choose the same pattern for all of them, since this will give a dull, boring result. Choose patterns which suit each other for a more exciting result. When the quilting is finished, trim the edges before adding binding.

Machine quilting

For machine quilting you should use a dual feeder. You should also find a good sitting position with your shoulders lowered. If you are planning a double bedspread and have problems with aching shoulders, it may be wise to have it quilted professionally. The larger the quilt is, the heavier it will be and the more difficult to pull through the machine when you are quilting.

A simple way to quilt is to sew ¼in from the seams. This is called 'stitching (or quilting) in the ditch'. When you sew two patches together and iron the seam allowance towards one of the patches, a 'ditch' is formed between those two pieces of fabric. Sewing along the seam on the fabric, which does not have the seam allowance underneath means that you are 'stitching in the ditch' which accentuates

the edge of a border or elements in the blocks. A special foot can be bought for most sewing machines which helps you to stay in the ditch when quilting. Increase the machine's stitch length beacuse too short a stitch length will leave you with a conspicuous seam with a hard appearance. With a stitch length of $^1/_8$–$^3/_{16}$in you will get a softer appearance and a seam which, from a distance, resembles hand quilting.

Hand quilting

Mark the quilting pattern with marking chalk, soluble felt tip pen or an ordinary 2B pencil. Always check beforehand that whatever you use for marking can be erased or will be removed by washing. If you are stitching in the ditch you don't need to mark the fabric.

If you haven't quilted in a frame before it may be wise to make a test piece on which to practise the stitches before getting going with a whole quilt. Use a thimble on your middle finger and let this finger control the needle on the top of the quilt. The quilt must not be too taut in the quilt frame, as this makes it difficult to control the needle. Control the fabric with the thumb of the same hand as the thimble finger and the middle finger of the other hand, which is under the quilt. Start in the centre of the quilt and work outwards towards the edges. Make a knot in the thread when you start, insert the needle into the centre of the quilt along one of the lines you have marked, and pull the knot through so that it disappears into the batting. When you begin to quilt, you will quilt over the thread that is inside the batting along the line, and this holds it a little more firmly.

When finishing off the thread or moving to the next pattern, make a double stitch through the batting and top. Go one stitch length back and make an ordinary quilt stitch through all three layers. This will 'lock' the quilt stitch and avoid round stitches. (The same should be done when you reach a corner if you, for example, quilt ¼in from the seam in a square.)

UNITS OF MEASUREMENT All measurements in this book are in inches because most patterns and equipment on the market at present use inches.

Hanging

If you want to be able to hang a quilt on the wall, you can make a hanging channel, which is attached before you sew on the binding. The following dimensions are for a hanging channel for competition quilts. You can make a narrower channel if you prefer. Cut a strip 8½in wide and as long as the width of the quilt. Fold in the ends, about ³/₈in, twice, press and stitch. Fold the channel double with the right side out and one edge protruding ½in beyond the other and iron flat. Place the raw edges together before pinning the hanging channel on the back of the quilt with the cut edges along the cut edges of the quilt. The channel should be centred, an equal distance from the edge of the quilt on both sides. Sew the channel in place. The lower part of the channel should be sewn in place by hand with invisible stitching along the fold made when you ironed the strip. This produces a slight bowing in the channel to provide space for the hanging rod. The front of the quilt will be flat when hanging.

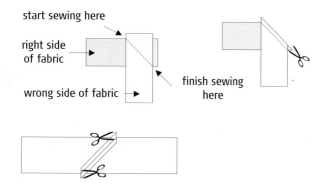

wrong side of quilt

Binding

There are many different ways of cutting and sewing binding. The method we use gives an attractive result. You can decide for yourself whether you want to cut the binding in straight strips or on the bias. If the batting is thick, or if for other reasons you feel that the binding is too narrow, you can cut the strips 2¼–2½in wide, but remember to increase the seam allowance to suit.

Cutting and assembling straight binding strips

Cut enough 2 × 45in (the full width of the fabric) strips to go round the entire quilt, including an allowance for joins. Join the strips diagonally as this is less conspicuous and also less bulky.

start sewing here

right side of fabric

wrong side of fabric →

finish sewing here

Trim the seam allowance to ¼in and iron the seams open. Trim off the 'ears' which protrude from the edges of the strip after the angled join has been finished. Fold the strip in half, wrong sides facing, and iron.

Cutting and assembling diagonal binding strips

We highly recommend diagonally cut binding, though many people find this is daunting and wasteful of fabric. If you are sewing wavy edges, diagonal cutting is often the only way to obtain a successful result, since it follows the edges more easily as you sew. However, the choice is yours! Lay out the fabric and cut 2in strips at 45 degrees to the weave. Cut enough to go all round the quilt plus a little extra for joins. The most practical length of fabric sheet is between 12 and 20in.

Join the strips by laying them right sides facing, and matching the cut ends. Sew a seam ¼in from the edge and press the seam open. Trim off the 'ears' that stick out at the edges of the strip. Fold the strip in half, wrong sides facing, and iron.

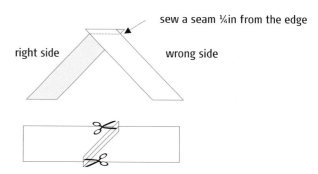

sew a seam ¼in from the edge

right side

wrong side

Adding the binding

When you sew on binding, it is wise to use a dual feeder on your machine. Lay the strip on the front with its raw edges against the raw edge of the quilt and starting about 8in from a corner. Start sewing about 4in from the end and stop $^3/_8$in from the corner. Lift the sewing machine foot with the needle down and continue the seam at a 45 degree angle out towards the corner.

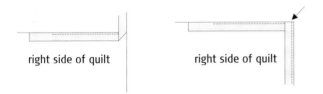

right side of quilt   right side of quilt

Lift the foot and fold the binding strip away from the corner at 45 degrees. Fold the tape down again so that it lies along the next edge of the quilt.

right side of quilt   right side of quilt

Sew all the corners in this way and finish off the seam when you are about 8in from the start of the binding. To join the binding place the end of the next strip (Part 2) over the end of the previous strip (Part 1) and mark the point about $^1/_8$in to the left of Part 2 with a pin. This produces a small amount of tension in the tape when you sew it together. (Note that the binding pieces are double but are drawn single here for simplicity.)

insert pin ⅛in to the left of Part 2

Part 1	Part 2

Fold the binding strips away from each other and place Part 2 with its right side facing and at 90 degrees to Part 1. The edge of Part 2 should be placed against the pin in Part 1.

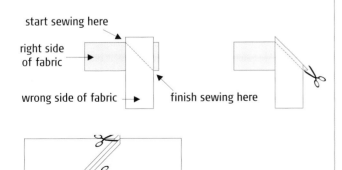

start sewing here

right side of fabric

wrong side of fabric → finish sewing here

Trim the seam allowance to ¼in and iron the seam open. Trim off the 'ears' which protrude from the edges of the strip after the angled join has been finished. Fold the strip in half, wrong sides facing, place it with the raw edge along the outer edge of the quilt and sew to complete attaching the binding.

Part 1	Part 2

Finally, fold the binding over to the back of the quilt and sew it down by hand using invisible stitching. To avoid too much mass at the corners, they should be folded the opposite way on the wrong side, compared with the right side.

Useful tips:

Whenever joining pieces, unless otherwise specified, use a ¼in seam allowance.

There are three ways of making a ¼in seam allowance:
- Some machines have a special setting called '¼in seam', which is used with an ordinary foot.
- Use an inch ruler and measure ¼in to the right of the needle and this mark with tape on the bed of the sewing machine.
- Use a ¼in sewing machine foot.

Seams should be ironed at each stage before continuing the assembly. Check that the size of the blocks is correct as you sew.

Factors for success

You probably won't always be completely satisfied with your patchwork quilts. Solutions are often found through trial and error. Try to turn negative experiences into positive ones, making use of the lessons as you progress as a quilter. Be on the lookout for attractive colour combinations, for example in works of art, interior decorating magazines, in fashions and in antique quilts. Another tip is to take photos and make notes of things you see. That way you will never run out of ideas and you will be more aware when choosing colours.

Let your quilts glitter with tiny jewels

In strip cartoons you can see how jewels in a treasure chest glitter. If you look closely, you will see that they are often mainly in pastel colours, each with a tiny white dot. The dot gives it the glittering effect, and you can get the same effect from your collection of fabrics. Fabric with a chalky white pattern produces quilts which gleam! Apart from this use, all white fabrics are often give the effect of 'holes' in a quilt. Instead of white it is probably better to use cream, ecru, pale lilac, pale yellow, pink, or similar shades.

There should be a greyish tinge

Pastels are favourites for many people, but they do need a little help, otherwise they may become a bit too candy-like. Grey is a fantastic colour for accentuating pastels. It also lends a pleasantly 'misty' atmosphere.

Shades of yellow

We haven't use a lot of yellow in these quilts, but pink grading into yellow (peach), blue grading into yellow (turquoise) and yellow grading into green can produce beautiful results.

Red is difficult

Red attracts attention. Many quilters use red only as 'rubies' in their quilts, but bright red can also be combined well with pale turquoise and other cold, light colours. Red then suddenly becomes a cold colour! You can see an example of red used this way in the 'Red, White and Blue' quilt on page 38.

Warm – cold

Decide beforehand whether your quilt is to give a warm or cold impression. Always remember to add something cold to a warm quilt and something warm to a cold quilt, as this provides balance and life.

Muted colours – clear colours

It is a good idea to mix colours a little, but finding the right combination isn't always easy. For example, a strong turquoise will be softened by a muted peach colour next to it – see the 'Golden Days' quilt, page 36.

Feminine – masculine

Tough, manly stripes combine well with pretty pink. The result is tension, contrast, Yin and Yang.

Old – new

It is exciting to use reproduction patterns or old shirts in combination with new fabric types. Just mix it!

Subdued greyish Japanese fabrics

Rowan's beautiful Japanese fabrics go well with slightly heavy grey, beige or brown. The fabrics add a little well-deserved glow to the languid colours, while the more colourful fabrics become more subdued. Combined the result is perfect!

Delicate – tough

If you want to sew a delicate quilt, you should include something tough here and there, or the quilt will appear sugary, rather than delicate.

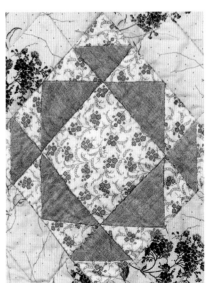

Avoid abrupt colour changes

Going straight from black to white can be too hard and brutal. Dark brown set against ecru is far better!

A surprise

A colour surprise (or several) will add interest to a quilt. By this we mean an unexpected colour combination. All the colours in a quilt don't need to match – perfection can be boring.

Contrasts

It is important to include some contrasts. Opposites in colours and patterns not only attract, but also emphasise each other. Typical contrasts can be:

Light – dark

Even if you are sewing a light quilt, you can include some dark fabrics. Completely pale quilts hardly get noticed!

Composing the quilt

Terminology:

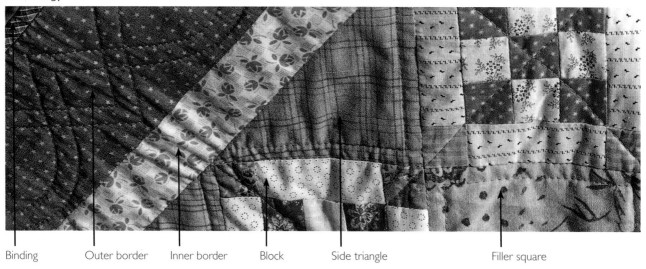

Binding   Outer border   Inner border   Block   Side triangle   Filler square

Design wall or door

Hang a flannel sheet or a sheet of batting over a Styrofoam sheet on a wall or door. Cut out the pieces of fabric that you are planning to use and place them on this background. The flannel or batting will hold the pieces so that they hang without pins. It is important to position your design wall somewhere where there are good light conditions, and where you can see the result in daylight, dusk and artificial light. There will always be variations and we want the quilt to look good in all types of light, if possible. This method allows you to see the whole quilt before you start sewing it together. The disadvantage is that it takes a lot of space, you have to cut and trim beforehand and you don't get as many left-over blocks.

Design floor

First sew about half of the blocks together, find the fabric for the filler pieces (and any sashing and border) and sew the rest of the blocks, taking the filler pieces into account. When all the blocks are finished, spread out the whole thing on the floor and place the blocks so that the colours are evenly distributed. The advantages of this method are that you can work very freely, you need less space and you often end up with left-over blocks which can be used later.

Block composition

When planning a project, it is a good idea to study the colours in a painting. For example, several of the quilts in this book are inspired by the paintings of the Swedish artist Carl Larsson (1853–1919). However, you can and should have plenty of freedom in your choice of colours. Don't think too much about matching colours within a single block, but rather that the colours match those of the adjacent block. Individually, the blocks might not be very attractive, but when you find a perfect filler, the overall result will be beautiful. Don't think too much – just sew! You can always recycle left-over four-patch blocks, nine-patch blocks, and so on.

The quilt as a whole

If your quilt consists of busy blocks with lots of colours and patterns, you will need more subdued filler pieces. If the main blocks are subdued, you can allow yourself more activity in the filler pieces. A good choice for sashing is a neat geometric (striped or dotted) or sinuous pattern. If you use large flowers in the filler areas, we recommend that you use sashing to separate the flowers. Large, complete flowers become an eye-catcher and it is best if the blocks play the major role in the quilt. By selecting the filler, sashing and border, you can decide the mood of the quilt, whether it is to be delicate, tough, light, dark, warm, cold, and so on. Choose whatever you find attractive.

The border should not look like the frame around a picture, but be an attractive finishing touch which unifies, calms and creates harmony. It should be a sort of common denominator for the whole quilt. Remember to mark the pieces of the quilt when you have finished arranging them, so that you will remember the composition when you move from the floor or wall to the sewing machine. You can either take a photo with a digital camera or use sticky labels, marking the rows 1, 2, 3 and so on, and the columns A, B, C. Then mark the blocks 1A, 1B, 1C, 2A, 2B, 2C, etc.

Tip!

Whichever composition method you use, before you sew the quilt together, it is a good idea to view it through a camera viewfinder (not a digital camera) or through a pair of binoculars turned the wrong way round; this gives a reduced view of the quilt, making it easier to see any unevenness or faults. You can also try looking through half-closed eyes or taking off your glasses if you wear them.

Dear Maggie

DESIGNED BY: Hilde Aanerud Krohg
HAND QUILTED BY: Hilde Aanerud Krohg
FINISHED QUILT SIZE: 20½ × 31in
FINISHED BLOCK SIZE: Window block, 4½in square

The inspiration for this quilt is a jacket designed by Cecilie Juvodden, whose Norwegian clothing brand is called Maggie Wonka. This beautiful white and grass green jacket is in a pretty brocade-like fabric with a paisley pattern. Grass green was a rather difficult colour for me to accept until I saw the jacket and it inspired me to sew this quilt.

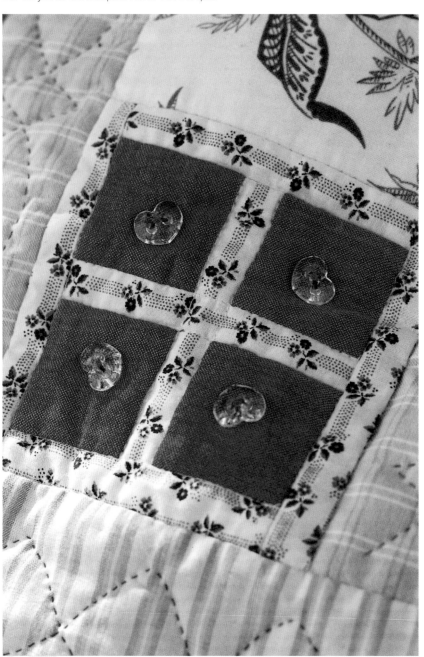

List of materials

Fabric for window blocks
• 12 window blocks: 16in (8in pale fabric and 8in green fabric)

Filler pieces, sashing and borders
• Filler pieces between the blocks: 12in (try to include any pattern elements)
• Vertical sashing: 10in
• Outer border on two short sides: 6in

About 12in of fabric for binding
Fabric for backing
Woollen batting

Cutting and assembly instructions
Window block
Cut and sew 12 blocks.

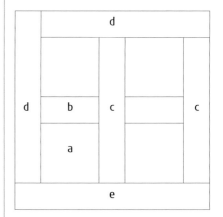

1 Choice of fabric for the 12 blocks
Each block consists of two colours: an intense grass green (with slight variations) in the window panes, and a light floral mini-print, in the frames. Each window pane also has a clear heart or flower shaped button.

2 Cutting the window block
• 4 pieces, 2 × 2in (a).
• 2 pieces, 1 × 2in (b).
• 2 pieces, 1 × 4in (c).
• 2 pieces, 1 × 4½in (d).
• 1 piece, 1 × 5in (e).

3 Assembling a window block

- Sew two strips consisting of one (a), one (b) and one (a).
- Sew these two strips together with a (c) between them. Make sure the (a) squares are lined up by checking along the edges, pin and sew together.
- Sew the frame together round the window starting with the other (c) along one side, a (d) along the next side, followed by another (d) and finally an (e).
- Trim the block to 5in square.

Filler pieces, sashing and borders

1 Choice of fabric

The tasteful grey-green for the filler pieces lends an element of peace to the more demanding grass green. I have carefully cut pieces of an Amy Butler fabric to include the branches. The sashings are pale blue plaid and stripes and the choice of a blue patterned binding gives a harmonious finish.

2 Cutting

- 9 pieces, 5 × 2½in, for the horizontal fillers between the blocks (f).
- 4 pieces, 2½ × 23in, for the vertical sashing (g).
- 2 pieces, 5 × 21in, for the outer border on the two short sides (h).

3 Assembly

- Sew vertical strips of window blocks with rectangles (f) in between as shown in the diagram. This gives a total of four blocks and three rectangles in each strip.
- Sew three strips like this.
- Sew the strips of blocks together with sashing (g) between and on each side.
- Finally, sew the outer border (h) to the short sides of the quilt.

Quilting

The blocks are button quilted with a button sewn in the centre of each window pane. The sashings and outer border are hand quilted using a grass green coloured thread. This was instead of the paisley embroidery I had dreamt of using in this quilt.

For the binding you need a strip 125in long. The method is described in Techniques on pages 14 and 15.

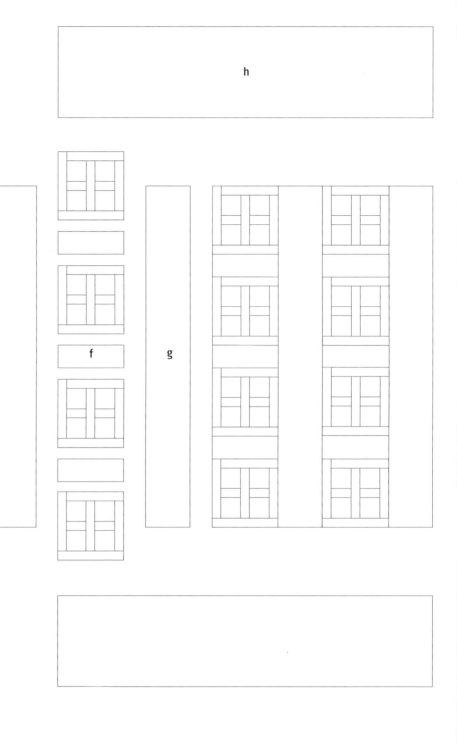

Edouard

DESIGNED BY: Hilde Aanerud Krohg
MACHINE QUILTED BY: Hilde Aanerud Krohg
FINISHED QUILT SIZE: 45 × 61in
FINISHED BLOCK SIZE: Cypress block, 6in square

This quilt was based on the colours in a painting by the French artist Vuillard (1868–1940). His first name was Edouard, almost the same as Rie's son, Edvard, for whom the quilt was made.

List of materials
Fabric for cypress blocks
- 28 cypress blocks: 24in light and 16in dark fabric

Fabric for side and corner triangles, sashing and outer border
- 64 side and corner triangles: 40in
- Sashing: 16in
- Outer border: 48in

About 16in of fabric for binding
Fabric for backing
Cotton batting

Cutting and assembly instructions
Cypress block
The cypress hedge grows cones that I think look like this block.

Cut and sew 28 blocks.

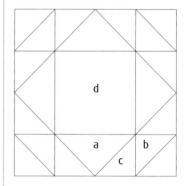

1 Choice of fabric for the 28 blocks
For all blocks except one, (a) and (b) are dark, while (c) and (d) are light. Or to put it another way, (a) and (b) have the leading roles and are therefore most conspicuous. The colours are turquoise, grey and deep red grading to lilac, pale green and sea green.

2 Cutting the cypress block
- 1 dark 4¼in square, cut diagonally to make 4 triangles (a).
- 2 dark 2⅜in squares, cut diagonally to make 4 triangles (b).
- 6 light 2⅜in squares, cut diagonally to make 12 triangles (c).
- 1 light 3½in square (d).

3 Assembling a cypress block

- Sew two triangles (c) to triangle (a). Sew three more rectangles in this way (a good alternative is to use Quick corners as described on page 8, or alternatively Flying Geese paper).

- Sew two of these units on opposite sides of square (d).
- Sew together the (b) and (c) triangles to make four squares. Sew a square to each end of the other two rectangles.

- Sew these two strips to the remaining sides of the square.

Side and corner triangles, sashing and outer border

1 Choice of fabric

The side triangles (e) and corners (f) are a grey, grained fabric with deep red flowers and turquoise leaves which match the blocks. There is a sashing of yellow fabric (g and h) and the border (i) has a turquoise paisley pattern.

2 Cutting

- 12 pieces, 10in square, cut diagonally to make 48 triangles (e).

- 4 pieces, 8¼in square, cut diagonally to make 16 triangles (f).

- 5 pieces, 2 × 42½in, for the vertical sashing (g).
- 2 pieces, 2 × 32in for the horizontal sashing (h).
- 2 pieces, 8 × 45in for the vertical outer border (i).
- 2 pieces, 8 × 47½in, for the horizontal outer border (j).

3 Assembly

- Sew diagonal block strips as shown in the diagram, with one (e) on each side of five blocks and one (e) and one (f) on the end blocks.
- Sew the diagonal strips together to form a vertical strip.
- Sew four of these block strips and sew on the last corner triangles (f). Trim the strips before sewing them together with a vertical sashing (g) between the strips and along the outside edges.
- Sew on the horizontal sashing (h).
- Sew the vertical outer borders (i) to the quilt.
- Sew the horizontal outer borders (j) to the quilt.
- Trim to 45 × 61in. (You could leave the trimming until you have finished quilting and are ready to attach the binding.)

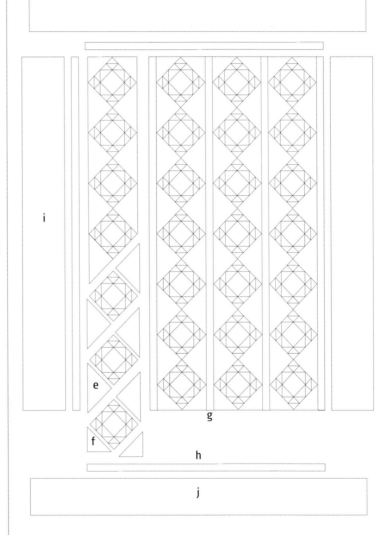

Quilting

The quilt is machine quilted with stitch in the ditch, ¼in into the sashing on each side. The border is quilted with a wide design.

Binding

For the binding you need a strip 230in long. The method is described in Techniques on pages 14 and 15.

Gorgeous Grey

DESIGNED BY: Hilde Aanerud Krohg
MACHINE QUILTED BY: Hilde Aanerud Krohg
FINISHED QUILT SIZE: 33 × 40in
FINISHED BLOCK SIZE: Framed nine-patch block, 5in square

Pastels are always georgeous. Shades of grey are almost as nice, and used next to pastels they make the pastels glow! My inspiration for this quilt is a painting by Vuillard entitled 'Still Life, Hydrangeas'. In it a royal blue crystal ball is on a table with a sea green vase, a surprisingly beautiful colour combination which I had to try in a patchwork quilt! Combining the grey with golden yellow I felt that the result was muted but not sad, and hence the title: Gorgeous Grey.

List of materials

Fabric for the framed nine-patch block
- 12 nine-patch blocks with frames:
  8in light, 8in medium, 8in dark fabric

Filler squares, side and corner triangles and borders
- 6 filler squares: 16in
- 14 side and corner triangles: 12in
- Inner borders: 4in
- Outer borders: 16in
- Corner squares in outer border: 6in

About 12in of fabric for binding
Fabric for backing
Cotton batting

Cutting and assembly instructions
Framed nine-patch block
Cut and sew 12 blocks.

		a		c
	b			

1 Choice of fabric for the 12 blocks
I decided on five dark and four light fabrics for the nine-patch blocks. The colours I used were deep turquoise, mauve and golden yellow, along with very pale fabrics in the frame and four light pieces in the nine-patch block itself. When it was finished I was really pleased with the combination of royal blue and sea green!

2 Cutting the framed nine-patch block
1½in strips for the strip sets. Cut a lot for the sake of variation! If you don't wish to sew strip sets, each block consists of:
- 4 pieces, 1½ × 3½in (a).
- 13 pieces, 1½ × 1½in (b) and (c).

  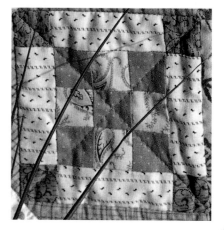

3 Assembling the nine-patch block

- Sew the strip set for the nine-patch blocks (see page 8). Finished dimensions: 3½in square.
- From the fabric, cut eight framing pieces four measuring 1½ × 3½in (a) and four 1½in square (c).
- Sew two (a) pieces on to the nine-patch block (one on each side).
- Sew a (c) square at each end of an (a) piece. Make two of these framework strips.
- Sew the two framework strips to the two block sides without framework.
- Trim the blocks to 5½in square.

Filler squares, side and corner triangles

1 Choice of fabric

Here we see the elegance of grey, with the stronger colours becoming more subdued. The filler squares are a beautiful linen fabric with gold printing. I didn't have quite enough of this fabric, so the triangles along the edge are made from a check fabric with some of the same grey and gold nuances.

2 Cutting

- 6 pieces, 5½in square, for the filler squares in the centre of the quilt (f).
- 3 pieces, 8in square, cut diagonally to make 12 side triangles (e).
- 1 piece, 6in square, cut diagonally to make 4 corner triangles (d).

3 Assembly

- Sew diagonal strips of blocks as shown in the diagram with squares (f) between each block and a side triangle (e) at each end. Sew a (d) on each strip which ends at a corner.
- Sew six strips like this.
- Sew the six strips of blocks and squares together, adding the last two triangles (d).

Inner and outer borders

1 Choice of fabric

The inner border is the same colour as the filler triangles, but in a paler tone. This unifies and makes the blocks more distinct, and creates a small space before the outer border. A blue-grey fabric with small white stars, is used for the outer border and the corner squares are in the same blue-grey shade, but with pretty sprigs of flowers.

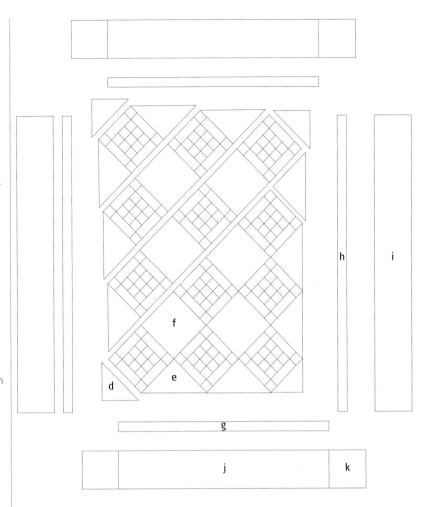

2 Cutting

- 2 pieces, 2 × 22¼in, for the horizontal inner border (g).
- 2 pieces, 2 × 32in, for the vertical inner border (h).
- 2 pieces, 4½ × 32in, for the vertical outer border (i).
- 2 pieces, 4½ × 24¾in, for the horizontal outer border (j).
- 4 pieces, 4½in square, for the corner squares in the outer border (k).

3 Assembly

- Sew the two horizontal inner borders (g) to the top and bottom of the quilt.
- Sew the two vertical inner borders (h) to the sides of the quilt.
- Sew the two vertical outer borders (i) to the sides of the quilt.
- Sew two corner squares (k) to each end of the horizontal outer borders (j) and then sew to the quilt.

Trim to 33 × 40in. (You could leave the trimming until you have finished quilting and are ready to attach the binding.)

Quilting

The quilt can be quilted either by hand or on a sewing machine. Use suitable thread in colours which suit the quilt. The outer border is quilted using a wide flowing design.

Binding

For the binding you need a strip 165in long. The method is described in Techniques on pages 14 and 15.

Summer Memories

DESIGNED BY: Hilde Aanerud Krohg
MACHINE QUILTED BY: Hilde Aanerud Krohg
FINISHED QUILT SIZE: 39 × 39in
FINISHED BLOCK SIZE: Double X blocks, 6in square

This pattern was inspired by a delightful summer scene painted by Swedish artist, Carl Larsson, called 'Ulf bathing on Bullerholm Island'.

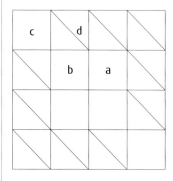

List of materials

Fabric for double X blocks

- 3 four-patch blocks: 8in light and 8in dark fabric
- 3 double X blocks: 8in light and 8in dark fabric

Filler squares, sashing and borders

- Filler squares: 16in
- Inner border: 8in
- Outer border: 20in

About 12 in of fabric for binding
Fabric for backing
Woollen batting

Cutting and assembly instructions
Double X block

Cut and sew 13 blocks.

1 Choice of fabric for the block

There are four colours in the block, and they are based on the colours in the Larsson picture and from my collection of fabrics.

The central four-patch block can be repeated if you want to sew strip sets.

2 Cutting the double X block

- 2 light and 2 dark 2in squares for the four-patch blocks (a) and (b), you can make 2in strip sets for these.
- 2 light 2in squares for the corners (c).
- 5 dark 2½in squares (d).
- 5 light 2½in squares (d).

You could use 'triangles on a roll' for the saw-tooth pieces.

3 Assembling the double X block

- Sew the two (a) and two (b) squares together to make a four-patch block. Iron the seams flat. You can vary the colours a lot here or you can use strip sets if you want several the same.
- Make the ten two-colour saw teeth squares (d) as follows. Place a light square on a dark one, right sides facing. Mark the diagonal on the lighter fabric using a pencil. Sew a ¼in seam each side of the pencil line. Cut the square in two exactly on the pencil line (see Fig 1). Open out and iron the seam against the dark fabric (light seam allowance under dark), and you have two saw teeth squares (Fig 2). Trim them to measure 2in square.

Fig. 1   Fig. 2

- Sew the saw-teeth squares together to make two pairs. It is important to refer to the block diagram so that the saw-teeth point in the right directions. It is very easy to get them the wrong way round! Sew them to the top and bottom of the four-patch block.
- Sew saw-teeth squares together in threes with a corner square (c) at one end. Sew these strips to the sides of the block, remembering that it is still important that the saw-teeth point the right way. Sew the required number of blocks, in this case 13 of them!
- Trim the blocks to 6½in square. It is a good idea to have a special ruler for this. Try to keep the saw-teeth sharp!

Filler squares combined with blocks

1 Choice of fabric
The choice of a pretty, flowered fabric with a pale yellow background was inspired by Larsson's summery picture.

2 Cutting
12 pieces, 6½in square, of filler fabric (e).

3 Composition
Use the floor, a table or design wall to arrange the blocks and filler squares so that the colours are evenly distributed. Remember that the blocks have a right and a wrong orientation!

4 Assembly
Sew together the blocks and filler fabric as shown in the diagram. Be precise – the saw-teeth should be sharp!

Inner and outer borders

1 Choice of fabric
A bright check inner border in orange/pink and a broad-striped outer border is particularly attractive. Sometimes I will add a corner square since stripes set at 90 degrees often seem a bit brutal and eye-catching. However, this wasn't necessary with the narrow stripes used in this quilt.

2 Inner border – cutting and assembly
- The border width is 1½in; measure the width of the quilt across the centre to find the length. The width of the quilt should be 30½in Cut two pieces, 1½ × 30½in (f).
- Sew on at the top and bottom (f).
- Once again, measure the quilt across the centre, now including the two inner border widths top and bottom. The quilt width should be 32½in. Cut two pieces, 1½ × 32½in (g).
- Sew on at the sides.

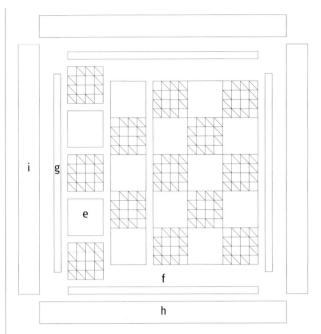

3 Outer border – cutting and assembly
- Measure and sew in the same way as for the inner border but this time the border width is 4½in, which is particularly suitable for using a commercially produced design when quilting them afterwards. The pieces should be:
- 2 pieces, 4½ × 32½in (h).
- 2 pieces, 4½ × 40½in (i).

Quilting
The quilt can be quilted either by hand or on a sewing machine. Use suitable thread in colours which suit the quilt. A wide flowing design was used for the border.

Binding
For the binding you need a strip 175in long. The method is described in Techniques on pages 14 and 15.

Midsummer Flower Garlands

DESIGNED BY: Hilde Aanerud Krohg
MACHINE QUILTED BY: Hilde Aanerud Krohg
FINISHED QUILT SIZE: 44¾ × 85in
FINISHED BLOCK SIZE: Four-patch blocks, 3in squares

Many of Carl Larsson's watercolours contain fantastic blues. I found them in the flowered fabric used for the outer border of this quilt, and I just had to make it into a bedspread for my daughter. Four-patch blocks on edge in long rows are striking; to me they are just like jewels on a necklace, but here they form garlands of flowers!

List of materials
Fabric for four-patch blocks
- 48 four-patch blocks: 12in light fabrics and 12in dark fabrics

Fabric for sashing, side and corner triangles, filler pieces and outer border
- 16in of dark neutral fabric for sashing
- 64in of pale neutral fabric for side and corner triangles
- 69in of striped fabric for filler pieces
- 71in of floral fabric for outer border

About 16in of fabric for binding
Fabric for backing
Cotton batting

Cutting and assembly instructions
Four-patch blocks
Cut and sew 48 blocks.

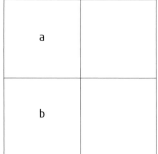

1 Choice of fabric for the 48 blocks
Pale, delicate pastels, are used in most of the four-patch blocks, a light and a dark in each set. Occasionally I have inserted some more powerful colours, including an orange fabric from Rowan, as a contrast to avoid a sugary effect. However, the orange turned out to be a bit too strident, so I sewed on a small lilac button to moderate the effect.

2 Cutting the four-patch block
Cut 2in strips and sort them into piles of light and dark.

3 Assembling a four-patch block
Choose a light and a dark strip and sew strip sets (see page 8) for the four-patch blocks (a) + (b). Trim to 3½in square.

Side and corner triangles, sashing and outer border

1 Choice of fabric

The side triangles are in a pale neutral lilac-grey fabric from Rowan. The sashing is in a darker neutral grey-green. These rather plain colours give a bit of life to the four-patch blocks. The filler fabric is a pale, narrow-striped fabric and the outer border is a violet coloured floral fabric inspired by Carl Larsson.

2 Cutting

- 23 pieces, 7in square, cut diagonally to make 92 side triangles, of which 90 are needed (c).
- 6 pieces, 3½in square, cut diagonally to make 12 corner triangles (d).
- 2 pieces, 4½ × 68½in, for filler pieces (with the stripes along their length) between the block strips (f).
- 6 pieces, 2 × 68½in, for the vertical sashing (e).
- 2 pieces, 2 × 30¾in, for the horizontal sashing (g).
- 2 pieces, 7 × 71½in, for the vertical outer border (h).
- 2 pieces, 7 × 44¾in, for the horizontal outer border (i).

3 Assembly

- Sew diagonal block strips as shown in the diagram, with one (c) on each side of the block and a (d) at the top and bottom.
- Sew the diagonal strips together to form a vertical strip.
- Sew three of these block strips and sew on the last corner triangles (d). Trim them before sewing them together with a vertical sashing (e) on each side of the strips of blocks.
- Sew on the striped filler fabric (f).
- Sew on the horizontal sashing (g).
- Sew the vertical outer borders (h) to the quilt.
- Sew the horizontal outer borders (i) to the quilt.

Trim to 44¾ × 85in. (You could leave the trimming until you have finished quilting and are ready to attach the binding.)

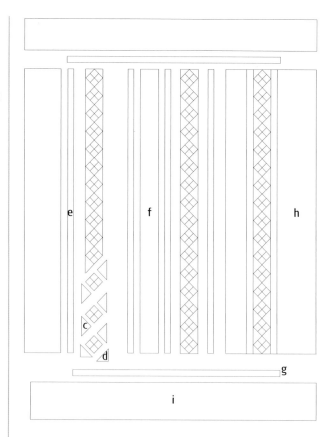

Quilting

The quilt is machine quilted using stitch in the ditch, ¼in into the sashing on each side. Two different border designs were used, one in the striped filler fabric and the other in the floral outer border.

Binding

For the binding you need a strip 280in long. The method is described in Techniques on pages 14 and 15.

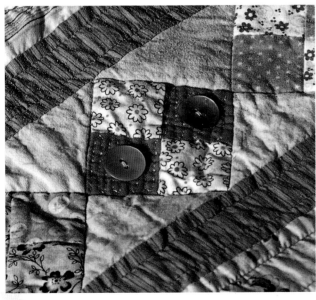

Golden Days

DESIGNED BY: Hilde Aanerud Krohg
MACHINE QUILTED BY: Hilde Aanerud Krohg
FINISHED QUILT SIZE: 28¾ × 38in
FINISHED BLOCK SIZE: Framed four-patch block, 4¼in square

I have a weakness for Carl Larsson's paintings, mainly for his colours, but also for his subjects and moods, festivals and daily life, indoors and outdoors, through all seasons of the year. This quilt came about after I saw a painting called 'Martina by the bonfire', which Larsson painted in 1908. I have borrowed his colours for this baby's pram cover which I have called 'Golden Days'. Its mood also reminds me of the pop music of the 80s and the result is this golden quilt.

List of materials

Fabric for the framed four-patch block
- 15 four-patch blocks: 4in of of pale yellow shirting fabric and 4in of pale blue floral fabric
- Frame: 12in turquoise and grass green fabric

Fabric for side and corner triangles and sashing
- Side and corner triangles: 12in
- Sashing: 12in

Fabric for outer border and corner triangles
- Outer border: 16in
- Corner triangles: 4in

About 12in of fabric for binding
Fabric for backing
Cotton batting

Cutting and assembly instructions
Framed four-patch block
Cut and sew 12 blocks.

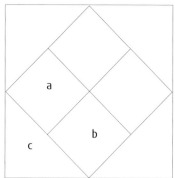

1 Choice of fabric for the 15 blocks
I have kept to the colours of the Swedish flag in the four-patch blocks, blue and yellow, but in fairly pale shades. For the frames I have chosen turquoise and grass green, in various shades from light to dark.

2 Cutting the four-patch block
- Cut enough 2in strips for 15 four-patch blocks and sort into piles of pale yellow and pale blue (a) and (b).
- 2 pieces, 3in square, cut diagonally to make 4 triangles for the frame (c).

- If you don't wish to sew a strip set, the block consists of: four pieces, 2in square, and two pieces, 3in square, cut diagonally.

3 Assembling the framed four-patch block
- Sew strip sets for the four-patch block (a) + (b) (see page 8); the finished block is 3½in square.
- Sew the longest side of the triangle (c) to the four-patch block, repeating the same on the opposite side. Then sew the two remaining sides.
- Trim the block to 4¾in square.

Side and corner triangles and sashing
1 Choice of fabric
I have used a a soft peachy fabric with small flowers for the side and corner triangles. This will subdue the liveliest pastel colours in the blocks. The sashing is golden yellow with white flowers which bring a little sparkle to the quilt.

2 Cutting
- 6 pieces, 7in square, cut diagonally to make 24 side triangles (d).
- 6 pieces, 3¾in square, cut diagonally to make 12 corner triangles (e).
- 4 pieces, 1¾ × 29½in, for the vertical sashing (f).
- 2 pieces, 1¾ × 22¾in, for the horizontal sashing (g).

3 Assembly
- Sew diagonal block strips as shown in the diagram, with one (d) on each side of three of the blocks and one (d) and one (e) on the other two.
- Sew three of these block strips and sew on the last corner triangles (e). Trim before sewing them together with the vertical sashing (f).
- Sew on the horizontal sashing (g).

Outer border with corner square
1 Choice of fabric
The border is the same shade as the side triangle, but a little stronger in colour. The corner squares are a pale peach coloured striped fabric as in Martina's blouse in the painting.

2 Cutting
- 2 pieces, 3½ × 38¼in, for the vertical outer border (h).
- 2 pieces, 3½ × 22¾in, for the horizontal outer border (i).
- 4 pieces, 3½in square, for the corner squares in the border (j).

3 Assembly
- Sew the two horizontal outer borders (i) to the top and bottom of the quilt.
- Sew corner squares (j) to each end of the vertical outer borders (h). Then sew to the sides of the quilt.
- Trim to 28¾ × 38in. (You could leave the trimming until you have finished quilting and are ready to attach the binding.)

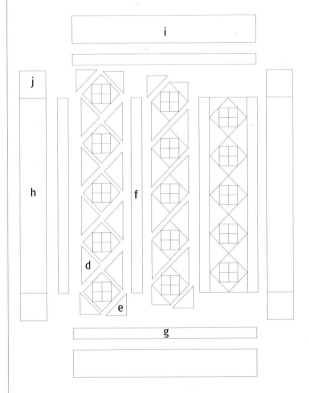

Quilting
The quilt can be quilted either by hand or on a sewing machine. Use suitable thread in colours which suit the quilt.

The machine quilting was done with thin cotton thread. First stitch in the ditch between the block and the side triangles. Sew ¼in within the ditch on each side of the sashing. Then quilt back and forth across the blocks. Finally, use a plastic template for the outer border pattern, marking it with a 2B pencil, and rotating it in the machine. All the rotating nearly made me giddy, so I suggest you use a simpler border!

Binding
For the binding you need a strip 155in long. The method is described in Techniques on pages 14 and 15.

Red, White and Blue

DESIGNED BY: Hilde Aanerud Krohg
QUILTED BY: Hilde Aanerud Krohg
FINISHED QUILT SIZE: 28¾ × 38in
FINISHED BLOCK SIZE: Framed four-patch block, 4¼in square

This is yet another quilt inspired by a Carl Larsson painting. I have to confess that my love for all things Swedish can, perhaps, be traced back to my Swedish great-grandmother. I have based this quilt on a well-known painting called 'Flowers on the Windowsill'. When I look at the picture I find myself thinking, What if there had been a quilt on the sofa in this painting? I feel that it should have had a little red in it to go with the beautiful pelargonium in the window.

List of materials
Fabric for the framed four-patch block
- 40 four-patch blocks: 10in of shirting fabric and 10in of pigeon blue fabric
- Frame, 20in red fabric

Fabrics for filler squares, borders, side and corner triangles
- Filler squares: 24in
- Side and corner triangles: 12in
- Inner border: 8in
- Outer border: 16in

About 12in of fabric for binding
Fabric for backing
Cotton batting

Cutting and assembly instructions
Framed four-patch block
Cut and sew 40 blocks.

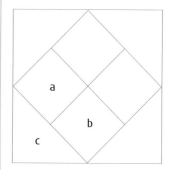

1 Choice of fabric for the 40 blocks
I have kept to red, white and blue in the four-patch blocks. The frame fabrics range from vivid red to peach and most have a white pattern to add a sparkle. The four-patch blocks are fairly similar, combining stippled pigeon blue fabric with shirting fabric.

2 Cutting the four-patch block
- Cut 2in strips for 40 four-patch blocks and sort into a pile of shirting fabric and a pile of blue fabric.
- 2 pieces, 3in square, cut diagonally to make 4 triangles for the frame.

If you don't wish to sew a strip set, the block consists of:
- 4 pieces, 2in square.
- 2 pieces, 3in square, cut diagonally to make 4 triangles.

3 Assembling the framed four-patch block

- Sew strip sets for the four-patch blocks (a) + (b) (see page 8); the finished dimensions are 3½in square.
- Sew the longest side of a triangle (c) to the four-patch block and do the same on the opposite side. Then sew triangles on to the two remaining sides.
- Trim the block to 4¾in square.

Filler squares and side and corner triangles

1 Choice of fabric

For the filler squares I have used a fabric containing sprigs of flowers, which to me epitomizes Carl Larsson – airy, light and summery! The side and corner triangles are made from pale turquoise with small red flower bouquets.

2 Cutting

- 28 pieces, 4¾in square, for filler squares (d).
- 6 pieces, 7in square, cut diagonally to make 24 side triangles (e), of which 22 are needed.
- 2 pieces, 3¾in square, cut diagonally to make 4 corner triangles (f).

3 Assembly

- Sew diagonal strips of blocks as shown in the diagram, filler squares (d) between each block and a side triangle (e) at each end. Sew an (f) on each strip which ends at a corner.
- Sew 12 of these units and trim ¼in from the block edge in the side triangles.

Inner and outer borders

1 Choice of fabric

A fairly strong blue fabric with red flowers is used for the inner border making the blue flowers in the filler fabric more conspicuous. The outer border is striped.

2 Cutting

- 2 pieces, 1¾ × 48½in, for the vertical inner border (g) (join the fabric).
- 2 pieces, 1¾ × 29in, for the horizontal inner border (h).
- 2 pieces, 3½ × 55¾in, for the vertical outer border (i) (join the fabric).
- 2 pieces, 3½ × 31½in, for the horizontal outer border (j).

3 Assembly

- Sew the two horizontal inner borders (h) to the top and bottom of the quilt.
- Sew the two vertical inner borders (g) to the sides of the quilt.
- Sew the two horizontal outer borders (i) to the top and bottom of the quilt.
- Sew the two vertical outer borders (j) to the long sides of the quilt.
- Trim to 38½ × 55¾in. (You could leave the trimming until you have finished quilting and are ready to attach the binding.)

Quilting

The quilt can be quilted either by hand or on a sewing machine. Use suitable thread in colours which suit the quilt. The machine quilting here has been done with thin cotton thread using stitch in the ditch between the block and the side triangles. The diagonal seams across the block are continued across the filler squares, producing a cross there. A hearts pattern was used in the outer border.

Binding

For the binding you need a strip 155in long. The method is described in Techniques on pages 14 and 15.

A Cup of Tea

DESIGNED BY: Hilde Aanerud Krohg
QUILTED BY: Hilde Aanerud Krohg
FINISHED QUILT SIZE: 48in square
FINISHED BLOCK SIZE: Teacup block, 8½in square

I created the first version of this design when I was asked to make a quilt after attending one of Kaffe Fassett's courses in the Hague. The title I gave it, 'A cup of tea for Kaffe', is a play on words, 'kaffe' being the Norwegian word for 'coffee'. It is described in the book 'Quilt Road', and consists entirely of Rowan fabrics. The original is now on tour, and I wanted to sew a new one which I could use in courses at home in Norway. It is slightly larger and redder than the original, and it is dedicated it to all my friends in sewing and quilting clubs, quilting shops, and on courses.

List of materials
Fabric for teacup blocks
- 32 backgrounds: 24in of light and 24in of dark fabric
- Teacup and handle: 12in
- Interior of cup: 12in light and 6in of medium fabric
- Saucer: 12in
- Shadow: 4in

Border
- Inner border: 18in
- Outer border: 14in

About 16in of fabric for binding
Fabric for backing
Cotton batting
Adhesive paper

Cutting and assembly instructions
Teacup block
Cut and sew 16 blocks.

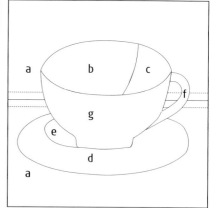

  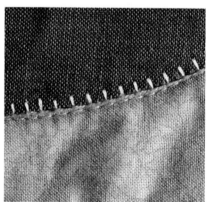

1 Choice of fabric for the blocks

The interiors of the teacups (b) and (c) are Rowan fabrics, pale blue with a slightly darker blue for the shadow. The teacups (f) and (g) are mainly red, patterned with large and small flowers, many of them also Rowan fabrics. Different one-coloured fabrics are used in the backgrounds (a). Note that in all the blocks the bottom half is a darker shade than the top. Each teacup has a red or brown saucer (d) with the shadow of the cup (e) in a darker shade.

2 Cutting the teacup blocks

Cut out a light and a dark background (a), 5¼ × 10in. Cut the various parts of the teacup by hand, the templates are on pages 114–115.

3 Assembling the blocks

• Put a light and a dark background, right sides facing, and sew them together. Iron the seam allowance open. Make 16 blocks. It is a good idea to make a plastic template for the whole teacup, showing where its parts are to be placed. Trace the outline of the cup (page 114) on to a plastic template sheet.

- Trace the teacup appliqué pieces (b)–(g) on the paper side of the adhesive paper, using the mirror-image parts on page 115. For parts which are partly concealed by others, add a 3⁄16in seam allowance, so as to avoid exposed raw edges. Cut out each part 1⁄4in outside the traced line on the paper itself. Iron it on to the wrong side of the chosen fabrics. Cut out the teacup parts exactly along the lines. Carefully remove the paper and place the parts, adhesive side down, on the background fabric.
- Fold the seam allowance of the shadow inside the cup (c) under, clipping the curve, and attach to the cup inside (b) by sewing it with invisible stitching. Place the teacup parts in alphabetical order using a plastic template to align the parts correctly. Iron in place and appliqué along the edges using buttonhole stitch. Use quilt stitching along the edge of (c).
- Trim the block to 9in square.

Inner border, outer border and corner squares

1 Choice of fabric

The inner border has pretty, pink flower sprays on a pale yellow background. It was so attractive that I found I had to make the inner border wider than the outer one. The outer border is turquoise with a red striped thread quilted into it. The corner triangles are a sea green Rowan fabric, like the outer border, and together they provide a good frame.

2 Cutting

- 2 pieces, 4 × 34½in, for the vertical inner border (h).
- 2 pieces, 4 × 41½in, for the horizontal inner border (i).
- 4 pieces, 3 × 41½in, for the outer border (j).
- 4 pieces, 3in square, for the corner squares (k).

3 Assembling the top edge

Arrange the blocks in four rows so that the colours are attractively distributed. Sew them together. Sew the vertical inner borders (h) to each side, and then the horizontal inner borders (i) to the top

and bottom. Sew the vertical outer borders (j) to the edges of the inner border. Sew the corner squares (k) to the ends of the horizontal outer borders and then and sew them to the quilt.

Quilting

The blanket can be quilted either by hand or on a sewing machine. Use suitable thread in colours which suit the quilt. Quilt the blocks using stitch in the ditch. Quilt round each teacup, taking care with your choice of thread, since you will be crossing two fabrics! Quilt over both inner and outer border with a simple flowing design.

Binding

For the binding you need a strip 210in long. The method is described in Techniques on pages 14 and 15.

Diamonds are Forever

DESIGNED BY: Hilde Aanerud Krohg
HAND QUILTED BY: Hilde Aanerud Krohg
FINISHED QUILT SIZE: 44 × 44in
FINISHED BLOCK SIZE: LeMoyne Star, 10¼in square

Most of these eight-pointed stars were made long before the quilt was completed. I had almost forgotten that they were in my drawer, but then I found an attractive sashing fabric and at the same time a pretty picture of a rustic kitchen in an interior decorating magazine. The rustic colours in both the fabric and the picture matched so well than it just had to be made into a quilt. I was planning to hand quilt it on an Easter holiday in a mountain cabin. Just before we left I lost my eternity ring, but on the way to the mountains we got a phone call saying that an honest soul had found my diamond ring in the snow! This was wonderful, and I am eternally grateful to Berit! There are nine stars in the quilt, and nine stones in the my ring, so the title just had to be 'Diamonds are Forever'.

List of materials

Fabric for eight-pointed star block
- 36 pieces, 3½in square, for the background squares
- 36 pieces, 5 × 3in, cut in two for the background triangles
- 72 pieces, 5¾ × 2¾in, for the star points

Fabric for the sashing
- 24 floral pieces, 3½ × 10¾in

Fabric for four-patch blocks
- 32 striped pieces, 1¾in square
- 32 pale pink pieces, 1¾in square

About 12in of fabric for binding
Fabric for backing
Woollen batting
9 heart-shaped mother-of-pearl buttons for the centre of each star

Cutting and assembly instructions
The whole quilt was hand sewn, but it can be done more simply if you wish. I have included some short-cuts which can be done on a machine.

Eight-pointed star block
The eight-pointed star pieces are hand sewn over thin card. The templates are on page 111. Trace the shapes on to the card and cut them out. You may be able to buy ready-made templates in quilting shops. The block, which consists of the star with square and triangular background pieces, looks like this:

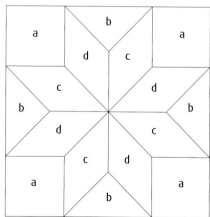

1 Choice of fabric for the block

I avoid stripes in these blocks as they can give a propeller-like effect and be too elaborate. Choose two contrasting fabrics for each star – light and dark, masculine and feminine, bright and muted, or any other combinations you like. One advantage of this block is that it is suitable for large-flowered fabrics, which are recommended. I have used the same background fabric for all the blocks: a pale checked fabric. Note that the blocks have a similar orientation, so it is a good idea to think about which of the diamonds have the most distinct colours when sewing them together, so that they either all have the same orientation or are random, as illustrated here.

2 Cutting the eight-pointed stars

The following is a description of how to cut the fabric pieces into squares, but if you cut obliquely to make diamonds and triangles, you will make better use of the fabric.
- 4 pieces, 3½in square (a).
- 4 pieces, 5 × 3in (b).
- 4 light pieces, 5¾ × 2¾in (c).
- 4 dark pieces, 5¾ × 2¾in (d).

3 Tacking (basting) the templates and assembling the block
- The method used to make the blocks is called English patchwork which is described on page 9. Tack (baste) the star pieces (c) and (d) to the paper templates.
- Sew the pieces together in pairs (c) + (d) (one of each of the fabrics), with fine backstitches. It is important that the seam allowances at the centre of the star all lie in the same direction (either clockwise or anticlockwise). This is why the seam allowance points in the same direction in both diamonds, allowing you to choose the direction in the centre, avoiding a build up of fabric on the wrong side.
- Tack (baste) the four squares to the paper templates in the same way. If you are sewing the whole quilt by hand, tack (baste) round the whole square. If you plan to sew the sashing by machine, you don't need to tack (baste) the seam allowance on the two outer sides.
- Sew a square (a) to each pair of star pieces (c) and (d), making four units:

These units are sewn together in pairs, as shown below:

- Tack (baste) the triangles (b), to the paper templates. If you are sewing the whole quilt by hand, tack (baste) round the whole triangle If you plan to sew the sashing by machine, you can leave the seam allowance on the long side.
- Sew a triangle into each unit (b).
- Sew the two halves together. Place a pin at the centre before you sew to help the points coincide. If they don't meet properly in the middle, just sew a button over the centre! All the stars in this quilt have heart-shaped buttons.
- Sew the last two triangles (b) to complete the block.

Sashing and border

The sashing surrounds the eight-pointed star blocks with four-patch blocks at the corners. If you want, you can sew these with a machine, though this quilt was sewn by hand over paper templates.

1 Choice of fabric
The sashing is a fantastic beige, rustic rose fabric, and the four-patch blocks are a pale pink, combined with a pale yellow, blue and beige striped fabric.

2 Cutting
Sashing rectangles
The finished length is the same as the side of the blocks and the width is the same as the corner squares. With seam allowances you will need 24 pieces, 3½ × 10¾in.

Four-patch blocks
The completed four-patch block is 3in square – the same size as the corner squares in the block. With seam allowances you will need 16 four-patch blocks, all of which are the same, made from:
- 32 striped pieces, 1¾in square.
- 32 pink pieces, 1¾in square.

Paper templates for sashing and four-patch blocks

Paper templates of fairly thick paper such as watercolour paper are are easily made. I put a blunt cutter wheel in my cutter and cut the paper as if it were fabric. Dead easy. The sashing template measures 3 × 10¼in and each block template measures 3in square. Tack and baste the fabric to the templates as before.

3 Assembly
- Sew a vertical strip of three star blocks, with sashing in between and at each end, as shown in the diagram. Sew three strips like this.
- Sew a vertical strip of four four-patch blocks with sashing between as shown in the diagram. Sew four strips like this.
- Sew all the vertical strips together to complete the top.

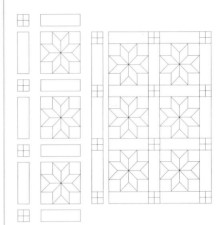

Quilting
The blanket can be quilted by hand or on a machine, but if the whole quilt is hand sewn, it is preferable to continue with hand quilting. I hand quilted using woollen batting, which is a pleasure to work with. I quilted all the seams with stitch in the ditch, and used a quilt border pattern on the sashing. Use suitable thread in colours which suit the quilt. When the quilting is complete, trim the quilt to 44 × 44in.

Binding
For the binding you need a strip 195in long. The method is described in Techniques on pages 14 and 15.

Lucky Retro

DESIGNED BY: Hilde Aanerud Krohg
HAND QUILTED BY: Hilde Aanerud Krohg
FINISHED QUILT SIZE: 19¼ × 22¼ in
FINISHED BLOCK SIZE: Four-leaf clover blocks, 3½ in square

When I was a girl in the 1970s I never tired of the patterns and colours which were in fashion in those days. Velvet frocks, retro fabrics and blouses with four-leaf clover patterns produce happy memories; Four hearts put together with their points touching make a four-leaf clover, which of course stands for luck! What more could anybody want?

List of materials

Fabric for the four-leaf clover block
- 48 hearts: 6in dark fabric
- 12 background pieces: 8in of pale fabric

Templates for the hearts
- Cut these from card using the pattern found on page 49, or alternatively buy a template in a quilting shop.

Fabric for inner border, outer border and corner squares
- Inner border: 4in
- Outer border: 10in
- Corner squares: 4in

About 4in of fabric for binding
Fabric for backing
Woollen batting
12 buttons for the centres of the four-leaf clovers – experiment with colours.

Cutting and assembly instructions
Most of this quilt is hand sewn, but the long seams can be sewn by machine to save strain on your arms.

Four-leaf clover block
Cut and sew 12 blocks.

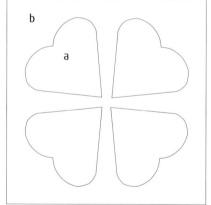

The backgrounds (b) are in pale blue, pale green, peach, turquoise and gold. The hearts (a) are black, navy blue and brown – and there is one green clover leaf at the request of my son, who said, 'But a four-leaf clover is green, Mummy!'

1 Cutting the four-leaf clover block
- Cut the background fabric (b) for the block, 4in square.
- 4 pieces, 2in square, for the hearts (a).

2 Basting the templates
- Pin the paper heart template to the fabric square and cut out leaving a ¼in seam allowance.

- Fold the fabric around the paper template, taking care to make even, sharp and flat folds. with a neat edge for appliquéing to the background fabric (b). Tack (baste) to hold.

- Place four hearts (a) with their points at the centre of the background fabric (b). Pin and appliqué on to the background fabric (b) using invisible stitching.
- Cut a slit in the background fabric and carefully remove the paper templates.
- Trim the block to 3¾in square.

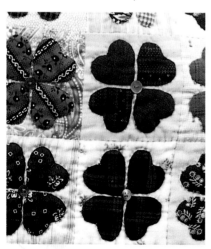

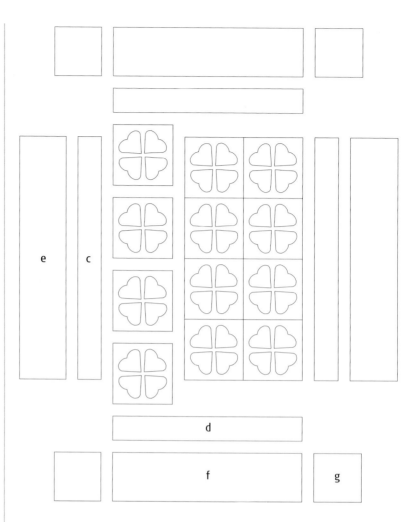

Inner and outer borders and corner squares
1 Choice of fabric
The inner border is a slightly rustic fabric in a grey shade, while the outer border is a bold black check fabric. The corner squares are golden yellow.

2 Cutting
- 2 pieces, 2 × 16½in, for the vertical inner border (c).
- 2 pieces, 2 × 13¼in, for the horizontal inner border (d).
- 2 pieces, 3½ × 16½in, for the vertical outer border (e).
- 2 pieces, 3½ × 13¼in, for the horizontal outer border (f).
- 4 pieces, 3½in square, for the corner squares (g).

3 Assembly – by machine if you wish
- Sew three vertical strips of four-leaf clover blocks as shown in the diagram.
- Sew the three strips of blocks together.
- Sew the vertical inner borders (c) to the sides of the quilt.
- Sew the horizontal inner borders (d) to top and bottom of the quilt.
- Sew the vertical outer borders (e) to the sides of the quilt.
- Sew corner squares (g) to each end of the horizontal outer borders (f).
- Sew the horizontal outer borders (g) + (f) + (g) to the top and bottom of the quilt.

Trim to 19¼ × 22¼in. (You could leave the trimming until you have finished quilting and are ready to attach the binding.)

Quilting

The quilt is hand quilted with stitch in the ditch along seams and close to the edges of the hearts. A rope pattern is used in the outer border. The quilt is filled with woollen batting which makes the hearts stand out after quilting. The buttons in the centres of each four-leaf clover also act as quilting, but are mainly for decoration.

Binding

For the binding you need a strip 95in long. The method is described in Techniques on pages 14 and 15.

Heart template

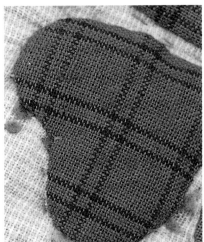

Puss in the Corner

DESIGNED BY: Hilde Aanerud Krohg
MACHINE QUILTED BY: Anne Fjellvær
FINISHED QUILT SIZE: 53in square
FINISHED BLOCK SIZE: Puss in the Corner block, 6in square

When you return home tired, beautiful fabrics like these from Amy Bulter will give you a lift. They are full of energy and colour, like so many of the Rowan fabrics which include this range. Some people feel that they are difficult to work with, but maybe this quilt design can make it easier to combine them with more familiar quilting fabrics.

Fabric for Puss in the Corner block
- 25 four-patch blocks: 12in light and 12in dark fabric

Fabric for filler squares, side and corner triangles and outer border
- 16 filler squares: 12in
- Side and corner triangles: 16in
- Outer border: 24in

About 12in of fabric for binding
Fabric for backing
Cotton batting

Cutting and assembly instructions
Puss in the Corner block

Puss in the Corner is an old party game in which all but one of the players have a corner of the room. Then everybody changes corners, while the player with no corner tries to get a vacant corner. You can see the corners clearly in the block, and if you like, you can try the game at home.

Cut and sew 25 blocks.

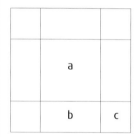

1 Choice of fabric for the block
I have used mainly Rowan and Amy Butler fabrics, with bold patterns and combined them with Japanese patterns, both light and dark. The dominant colours are pink, brown, blue and green.

2 Cutting a Puss in the Corner block
Cut light and dark strips 2in and 3½in wide and sort them into two separate piles. If you don't wish to sew a strip set, the block consists of:
- 1 piece, 3½in square (a).
- 4 pieces, 3½ × 2in (b).
- 4 pieces, 2in square (c).

3 Assembling Puss in the Corner

Sew the strip set for the nine-patch block (see page 8). If necessary, trim the block to 6½in square.

Filler squares, side and corner triangles

1 Choice of fabric

A broad-striped bolster-like fabric was used for the filler squares. The fabric is rather thick and has pink stripes on a white background. The same fabric, but with a pale green background, was used for the side and corner triangles.

2 Cutting

- 16 pieces, 6in square, cut for the filler squares at the centre of the quilt (d).
- 4 pieces, 10in square, cut diagonally to give a total of 16 triangles (e).
- 1 piece, 8¼in square, cut diagonally to give a total of 4 triangles (f), one for each corner.

3 Assembly

- Sew diagonal strips of blocks with squares between, a side triangle at each end, and a triangle at each corner as shown in the diagram.
- Sew nine strips like this.
- Sew the strips of blocks together and add the last two corner triangles.

Outer border

1 Choice of fabric

The flowered outer border fabric is from Amy Butler and contains the same colours as the side and corner triangles.

2 Cutting

- 2 pieces, 5 × 53in, for the horizontal outer border (g).
- 2 pieces, 5 × 43in, for the vertical outer border (h).

3 Assembly

- Sew the two vertical outer borders (h) to the sides of the quilt.
- Sew the two horizontal outer borders (g) to the top and bottom of the quilt.
- Trim to 53in square. (You could leave the trimming until you have finished quilting and are ready to attach the binding.)

Quilting

The quilt is machine quilted using stitch in the ditch, with the stitching continuing across the filler squares so that the Puss in the Corner pattern is repeated in the quilting. The outer border was quilted using a simple flowing rope design.

Binding

For the binding you need a strip 230in long. The method is described in Techniques on pages 14 and 15.

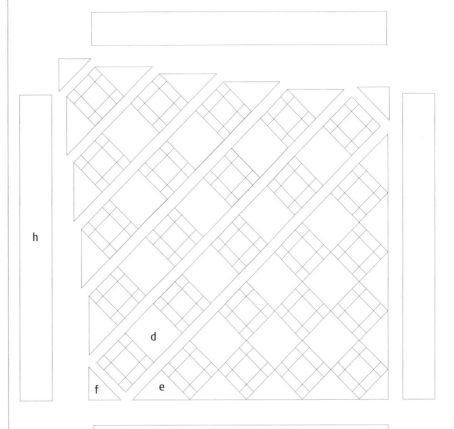

It Takes Two

DESIGNED BY: Hilde Aanerud Krohg
MACHINE QUILTED BY: Hilde Aanerud Krohg
FINISHED QUILT SIZE: 56½ × 81¾in
FINISHED BLOCK SIZE: Puss in the Corner block, 6in square

This is Puss in the Corner Part 2, using surplus blocks from that quilt with new ones with slight variations. The blocks are set in slightly more masculine surroundings, with dark Japanese fabric used for the filler squares, and the result is a completely different impression. The quilt has been decorated with space dyed ribbons running along its length which brighten up the quilt.

List of materials

Fabric for Puss in the Corner blocks
- 40 Puss in the Corner blocks: 16in light and 16in dark fabric

Fabrics for filler squares, side and corner triangles and outer border
- 28 filler squares: 24in
- 26 side and corner triangles: 16in
- Outer border: 32in

About 18in of fabric for binding
Fabric for backing
Cotton batting
Ribbon instead of vertical sashing

Cutting and assembly instructions
Puss in the Corner block
Cut and assemble 40 blocks in the same way as for the quilt on page 50. I simply used leftover blocks from that quilt, plus three Cypress blocks left over from the Edouard quilt, as they are the same size.

Cypress block
Cut and assemble three Cypress blocks in the same way as described on pages 24 and 25.

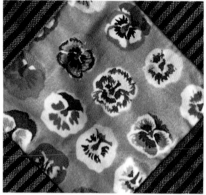

Filler squares, side and corner triangles

1 Choice of fabric

A dark green Japanese fabric with red dots was used for the filler squares and the surrounding triangles within the outer border.

2 Cutting

- 28 pieces, 6½in square, for the filler squares (d).
- 6 pieces, 10in square, cut diagonally to make a total of 24 side triangles (e), of which 22 are needed.
- 1 piece, 8¼in square, cut diagonally to make a total of 4 triangles (f), one for each corner.

3 Assembly

- Sew diagonal strips of blocks with squares (d) between each block, a side triangle (e) at each end and a corner triangle (f) at each corner, as shown in the diagram on page 55.
- Sew twelve strips like this.
- Sew the strips together and add the last two corner triangles (f).

Outer border

1 Choice of fabric

A wide striped Amy Butler fabric was used for the outer border. The base colour in the stripes is a slightly lighter, more vivid green than the filler squares.

2 Cutting

- 2 pieces, 7 × 57in, for the horizontal outer border (g).
- 2 pieces, 7 × 68¼in, for the vertical outer border (h).

3 Assembly

- Sew the two vertical outer borders (h) to the sides of the quilt.
- Sew the two horizontal outer borders (g). to the top and bottom using slightly longer stitches, since you are going to unpick them and insert ribbons here later on.
- Trim to 56½ × 81¾in. (You could leave the trimming until you have finished quilting and are ready to attach the binding.)

Quilting

The quilt is machine quilted using stitch in the ditch, with the stitching continuing across the filler squares so that the Puss in the Corner pattern is repeated in the quilting. The stripes in the Amy Butler fabric run across the border and the machine quilting repeats the stripes, but lengthwise.

Attaching ribbon

The ribbon is tacked (basted) on after the front is completed. The ends of the ribbons are tucked under the outer border. Unpick the stitches, push the end of each ribbon in and re-sew the whole seam, using a machine, working from the wrong side. Quilt along the whole ribbon after the batting and backing fabric have been added, removing the tacking (basting) stitches at the end.

For the binding you need a strip 300in long. The method is described in Techniques on pages 14 and 15.

h

d

f   e

g

Stargazer

DESIGNED BY: Hilde Aanerud Krohg
QUILTED BY: Hilde Aanerud Krohg
FINISHED QUILT SIZE: 40¾ × 52¼in
FINISHED BLOCK SIZE: Ohio Star, 5in square. Four-patch block, 3in square.

This quilt was made for my oldest son, Axel, because he loves the night sky and I love four-patch blocks. I often use four-patch blocks in my quilts, usually measuring 3in square. Sew sets of strips if you like, and have recycling in mind.

List of materials

Fabric for four-patch blocks
- Various light fabrics: 24in in all, cut into 45 strips 2in wide
- Various dark fabrics: 24in in all, cut into 45 strips 2in wide

Fabric for the Ohio Star blocks
- Various light fabrics: 16in
- Various dark fabrics: 16in

Fabric for the sashing and side and corner triangles
- Sashing: 16in
- Side and corner triangles: 20in

About 16in of fabric for binding
Fabric for backing
Cotton batting

Cutting and assembly instructions
Four-patch block
Cut and sew 45 blocks.

Choice of fabric for the blocks
Use warm colours such as brown, blue, yellow, etc, with one light and one dark colour in each block, or a strong colour with a paler shade.

1 Cutting the four-patch blocks
Cut sets of 2in strips, one pile of light and one pile of dark.

2 Assembling the four-patch block
Sew a strip set for the four-patch block (a) + (b) (see page 7); the finished dimension is 3in square.

Ohio Star block
Cut and sew 14 blocks.

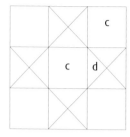

Choice of fabric for the Ohio Star
Warm colours, brown, blue, camel, etc. Try to find backgrounds which are dark enough to match the border, and star colours which contrast with the background but don't stand out too much.

1 Cutting the Ohio Star block
- 4 light pieces, 2⅜in square (c).
- 1 dark piece, 2⅜ in square (c).
- 2 dark pieces, 3⅛in square (d) cut diagonally to make 8 triangles.
- 2 light pieces, 3⅛in square (d) cut diagonally to make 8 triangles

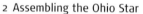

2 Assembling the Ohio Star
The Ohio Star is really a nine-patch block but with four of the nine pieces containing an hourglass made from triangles.

Start by making the hourglass squares
- Sew the short side of a light triangle (d) to the short side of a dark triangle (d).
- Repeat, then sew them together to make a square.
- Make four of these squares. Then sew the star together using four light and one dark square (c) as a nine-patch block (see page 8).

Side and corner triangles, sashing and filler squares
1 Choice of fabric
The side triangles are in a neutral colour – a grey and pink striped Rowan fabric. The sashing is a red fabric with stripes of white flowers. The outer border consists of Ohio stars and filler squares in the same colour tones as the star backgrounds.

2 Cutting

- 20 pieces, 7in square, cut diagonally to make 80 triangles (e).
- 10 pieces, 3½in square, cut diagonally to make 20 corner triangles (f).
- 6 pieces, 1¾ × 38½in, for the vertical sashing (g).
- 2 pieces, 1¾ × 29¼in, for the horizontal sashing (h).
- 14 pieces, 5¾in square, for the corner squares in the outer border (i).
- 14 Ohio Stars in the outer border.

Assembly

- Sew diagonal block strips with one (e) on each side of the block and one (f) at the top and bottom as shown in the diagram.
- Sew the strips together to form a vertical strip.
- Sew five of these block strips and sew on the last corner triangles (f). Trim before sewing them together with the vertical sashing (g).
- Sew on the horizontal sashing (h).
- Sew three stars and four filler squares (i) together to form a vertical outer border. Make two of these strips and sew them to the sides of the quilt.
- Sew four stars and three filler squares (i) together to form a horizontal outer border. Make two of these strips and sew them to the top and bottom of the quilt.
- Trim to 40¾ × 52¼in. (You could leave the trimming until you have finished quilting and are ready to attach the binding.)

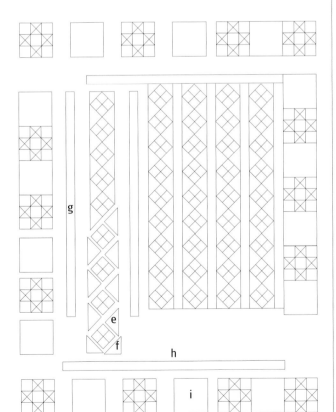

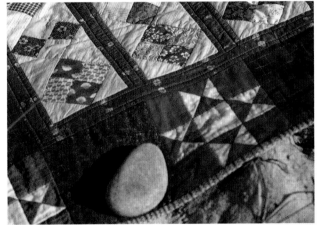

Quilting

The quilt is machine quilted using stitch in the ditch, ¼in along each side of all the sashing.

Binding

For the binding you need a strip 210in long. The method is described in Techniques on pages 14 and 15.

Star Boat

DESIGNED BY: Rie Norum
HAND QUILTED BY: Anne Fjellvær
FINISHED QUILT SIZE: 66 × 81½in
FINISHED BLOCK SIZE: Star block, 12in square. Indianapolis block, 3½in square

This is all summer and sun. The quilt was created in the hottest part of the year, with high temperatures and brilliant colours outside, which are reflected in the choice of bright hues. The large stars in the quilt resemble a LeMoyne Star block, but the diamonds have been cut to form a central circle with the colours alternating with the outer points. The small blocks in the sashings are identical and are a simplified version of the 'Indianapolis' block, from Jane Stickle's quilt of 1863. The green background fabric is the same both in the star blocks and in the small blocks in the sashings. The star blocks contain reproduction fabrics in various shades of blue as well as light shirting fabrics with elements of red or pink. The sashing between the blocks is sewn from two different fabrics, a pink striped one and a shirting fabric.

The quilt is hand quilted using the Bishop's Fan quilt pattern.

List of materials

Fabric for star blocks

- 20 pieces of blue fabric, 10 × 12in, in various shades
- 20 pieces of light shirting fabric, 10 × 12in, with print in various red and pink shades
- About 67in of green fabric for the background

Fabric for Indianapolis blocks

- About 28in of light fabric
- About 16in of green fabric

Fabric for sashings

- About 80in of pink fabric
- About 32in of light shirting fabric

About 20in of fabric for binding
Fabric for backing
Cotton batting

Spray adhesive
Glue stick
About 3ft of freezer paper

The block in the framework is enlarged and inserted in the backing fabric.

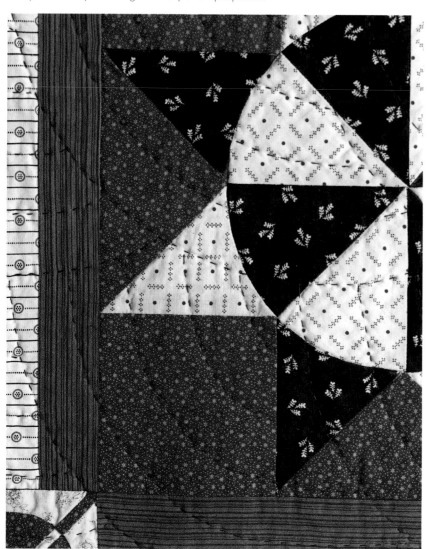

Cutting and assembly instructions Star block

The template for the star block is on page 113. Enlarge the template by 200 per cent so that it measures 12in square. Cut and sew 40 blocks.

1 Cutting a star block

- Cut four 3 × 6in rectangles in light fabric (a) and then cut each diagonally at 45 degrees (see the diagram below) to give two triangles, eight in all. Cut four rectangles in dark fabric (b) in the same way to give eight triangles.
(The whole quilt uses 160 light and 160 dark triangles.)

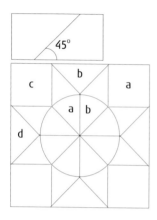

- 4 pieces, 4in square, for corners (c). (80 for the whole quilt.)
- 1 piece, 6½in square, cut diagonally, to make 4 triangles, (d). (80 for the whole quilt.)

2 Assembling the Star block

- Using the eight (a) and (b) triangles, sew a pinwheel block. The pinwheel inside the circle can be sewn simply and accurately using the technique Piecing using freezer paper on page 11. See also the detailed description of making a pinwheel block in 'The Wheels on the Bus go Round and Round' on page 104. Cut out the block template as shown below:

- Lay aside the pinwheel block while you complete the outer edge of the block. Make a fold along all the lines on the outer edge of the star block template. Begin at one corner (c) and using the same technique sew around.

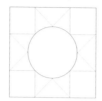

- When you have sewn together all the parts and only have the last seam to do, mark where the seam is to be on the back of the last two pieces.
- Peel your work away from each side of the freezer paper, place the parts right sides facing, pin and sew them together. Iron the freezer paper again. You are now ready to sew the pinwheel block to the outer edge. Follow the description of reverse appliqué by machine on page 10. Make sure that part (a) is laid opposite part (b) and that the seams meet when you glue the pinwheel block together.

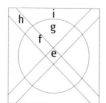

- Sew 20 blocks like this. Trim the blocks to 12½in square.

Indianapolis block and sashings

The template for the Indianapolis block is on page 112.

Cutting the Indianapolis block

- Cut 1 piece, ¾in square, for the centre of the block (e).
- Cut 4 pieces, ¾ × 1¾in, for the cross (f).
- Cut 4 pieces, 1¾in square, for circle (g).

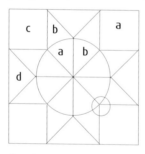

If you are going to use the same fabric in all the blocks, you can save time by sewing strip sets as described on page 8 (then you can leave out the first three steps above and cut strips from the whole length of the fabric instead).

- Cut 4 pieces, ¾ × 2in, for the corner cross (h).
- Cut a piece, 4¾in square, which is cut diagonally twice, to make 4 triangles (i).

Assembling the Indianapolis block

- Sew together a nine-patch block from one part (e), four parts (f) and four parts (g). Sew a total of 30 blocks of this type. The nine-patch block will measure 3¼in square.
- Sew the outer edge of the block using freezer paper as for the star block.
- Sew a total of 30 blocks.
- Trim the blocks to 4in square.

g	f	g
f	e	f
g	f	g

Cutting the sashings

- 49 pieces, 1½ × 12½in, for sashings (h).
- 98 pieces, 1¾ × 12½in, for sashings (i).

Assembling the sashings

Sew together one part (h) and two parts (i) to form a rectangle, 4 × 12½in.

i
h
i

Assembling the quilt
- Sew the star blocks to the sashings in horizontal columns as shown in the diagram below.
- Do the same with the sashings and Indianapolis blocks. Now sew the strips together and iron the seam allowances away from the blocks.

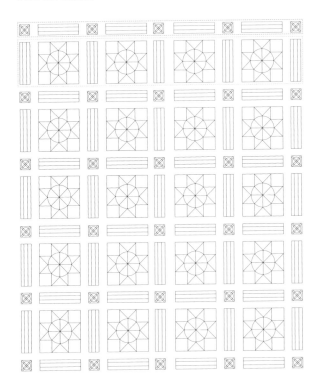

Quilting
The quilt was hand quilted with large stitches to emphasise the slightly rough appearance. Dark brown silk thread was used which provides an attractive contrast with the fabrics. The quilting pattern is called Bishop's Fan and covers the entire quilt. Mark the pattern with marking chalk and quilt along rows. It is a good idea to mark the height of each row so that they don't become crooked.

Binding
For the binding you need a strip 310in long. The method is described in Techniques on pages 14 and 15.

Star Boat Tablecloth

DESIGNED BY: Rie Norum
HAND QUILTED BY: Rie Norum
TABLECLOTH DIMENSIONS: 14 × 32in
FINISHED BLOCK SIZE: Indianapolis block, 3½in square

The Indianapolis blocks used in the sashings of the Star Boat quilt were the result of a long, drawn-out process. In all I sewed 12 blocks in various fabrics before I found one which looked right. The remaining 11 blocks became the starting point for a new project. The plan was for the tablecloth to match the quilt but that the same fabrics should not be used again – except for the green fabric. The blocks were moved around for several days before they finally fell into place. The cloth is quilted with Bishop's Fan – the same pattern as the quilt, but in a smaller version. The light coloured binding connects with the light central section and as a result the cloth appears light, in spite of its dark frame.

List of materials
Fabric for the Indianapolis blocks
- 11 pieces, 10 × 12in, in a variety of light coloured fabrics.
- 12in of green fabric

Fabric for the four-patch blocks and border
- Four-patch blocks: 8in of light shirting fabric
- Border: 10in of red fabric

About 8in of fabric for binding
Fabric for backing
Batting

Spray adhesive
Glue stick
About 12in of freezer paper

Cutting and assembly instructions
Indianapolis block
The template for the Indianapolis block is on page 112.

1 Cutting the Indianapolis block
Follow the instructions for cutting the Indianapolis block given for the Star Boat quilt, page 60.

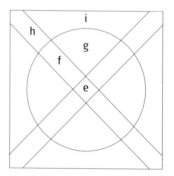

You need to cut:
- 11 (e) pieces.
- 44 (f) pieces.
- 11 (g) pieces.
- 44 (h) pieces.
- 11 (i) pieces.

If you plan to use the same fabric in all the blocks you can save time by sewing strip sets (see page 8 and the Indianapolis block, page 60).

2 Assembly

Follow the same procedure as described for the Indianapolis block.

- Sew a total of 11 blocks.
- Trim the blocks to 4in square.

Four-patch blocks

1 Cutting

- 40 pieces, 2¼in square, for four-patch blocks.

2 Assembly

- Sew together the squares to make ten four-patch blocks (see page 7).
- Sew the Indianapolis blocks to the four-patch blocks in rows as shown in the diagram below.

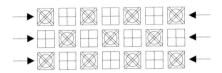

- Sew the rows together and iron the seam allowances away from the blocks.

Border

1 Cutting

- 2 pieces, 2 × 25in, for the side border fabric (j).
- 2 pieces, 4 × 14in, for the top and bottom border fabric (k).

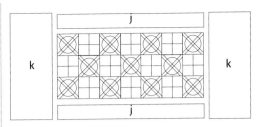

2 Assembly

- Sew the two side borders (j) to the central section.
- Sew the two remaining borders (k) to the top and bottom of the cloth.
- Trim to 14 × 32in. (You could leave the trimming until you have finished quilting and are ready to attach the binding.)

Quilting

The tablecloth is hand quilted with large stitches using a smaller version of the Bishop's Fan pattern as in the Star Boat quilt. Dark brown silk thread was used to provide an attractive contrast with the fabrics. Mark the pattern with marking chalk and quilt along the rows. It is a good idea to mark the height of each row so that they don't become crooked.

Binding

For the binding you need a strip 105in long. The method is described in Techniques on pages 14 and 15.

All in a Row

DESIGNED BY: Rie Norum
MACHINE QUILTED BY: Rie Norum
TABLECLOTH DIMENSIONS: 26 × 50in

When beautiful fabrics are used in large sections they really come into their own. When I found this floral fabric I just had to make something with it right away. I had inherited an antique table which needed a new tablecloth. The border is wide and conspicuous and this emphasises the character of the tablecloth. It is easy to adjust the width and length of the cloth to suit your purposes.

I don't always buy clothes to wear them. When I came across a blouse decorated with tiny metal sequins, I felt a new project coming on. The blouse quickly lost all its decoration and when the tablecloth was finished the sequins were sewn on by hand at the intersections of the diamond quilting pattern.

- Sew the two remaining end edges (d) to the top and bottom of the cloth.
- Trim to 26 × 50in. (You could leave the trimming until you have finished quilting and are ready to attach the binding.)

Quilting

The cloth is hand quilted using stitch in the ditch and silk thread. The quilt border patterns are transferred to the fabric using plastic templates and marking chalk.

Binding

For the binding you need a strip 165in long. The method is described in Techniques on pages 14 and 15.

If you want to add sequins, it is best to wait until after washing the quilt and then sew them on by hand using backstitching in the quilting seams.

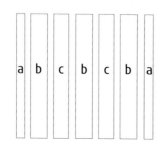

List of materials

- 18in of fabric for the three rows (b) in the central section
- 10in of fabric for the two rows (c) in the central section
- 8in of fabric for side edges (a)
- 18in of fabric for end edges (d)

- About 6in of fabric for binding
- Fabric for backing
- Batting

Cutting and assembly instructions

1 Cutting

- Cut two pieces, 2½ × 35in, for the side edges of the cloth (a).
- Cut three pieces, 5 × 35in, for the rows in the central section (b).
- Cut two pieces, 4½ × 35in, for the rows in the central section (c).
- Cut two pieces, 8 × 26in, for the end edges (d).

2 Assembly

- Sew the rectangles together in the following order: (a) + (b) + (c) + (b) + (c) + (b) + (a).

Buttoned up Bag

DESIGNED BY: Rie Norum
SEWN BY: Rie Norum

When a friend of mine came home from holiday with a beautiful shopping bag on her arm, it didn't take long before I was in my sewing room. After an evening of drawing and basting, with much trial and error, this shopping bag saw the light of day. I wanted both the strap and the bag itself to be adjustable. When you have small children running in all directions, it is practical to be able to sling a bag over your head and shoulder leaving both hands free. To allow for larger loads, there is a press stud in the bottom of the bag which will provide more carrying capacity when opened.

Why should buttons all be the same? Just go wild with the buttons and add your own personal touch to the bag. Just remember to choose buttons of the same size.

List of materials
Large shopping bag
- 36in of fabric for the bag
- 6in of fabric for the outside top edge
- 6in of fabric for the inside top edge
- 36in of fabric for the lining
- 6in of fabric for the shoulder strap
- 6in of fabric for the binding on the shoulder strap
- 10in of iron-on interfacing for the edge
- 36in of iron-on woven interfacing to reinforce the bag fabric if it is thin
- 3-4 buttons, depending on size and how many there is room for on the bag edge
- 1 press stud
- Buttonhole foot
- If you choose a heavy fabric like denim you will need a jeans needle

Small shopping bag
- 30in of fabric for the bag
- 6in of fabric for the outside top edge
- 6in of fabric for the inside top edge
- 30in of fabric for the lining
- 6in of fabric for the shoulder strap
- 6in of fabric for the binding on the shoulder strap
- 10in of iron-on interfacing for the edge
- 30in of iron-on woven interfacing to reinforce the bag fabric if it is thin
- 3-4 buttons, depending on size and how many there is room for on the bag edge
- Buttonhole foot
- If you choose a heavy fabric like denim you will need a jeans needle

Cutting and assembly instructions

1 Cutting the fabric and lining

- Cut circles of the fabric, lining fabric and woven interfacing. (If you are using a slightly thicker fabric it won't be necessary to reinforce it.) The diameter of the circle for the large bag is 34in and for the small bag 28in. The seam allowance is included in the dimensions. Draw lines across the diameter, at right angles, to mark the centre and to quarter the circumference. The press studs are located 4in each side of the centre of the larger bag.

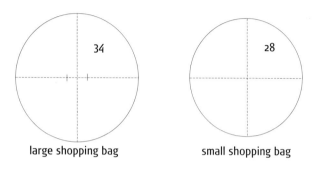

large shopping bag   small shopping bag

- For the top edge of the bag, cut 23½ × 4½in rectangles of fabric, lining and woven interfacing. (The edge of the larger bag is made from two contrasting strips of fabric sewn together to make the rectangle.)
- Cut two 2 × 36in rectangles of fabric and woven interfacing for the strap.
- Cut a 2 × 45in strip of fabric for binding on one edge of the shoulder strap. If you want to bind both edges, you will need two of these strips.

2 Assembling the outside of the bag

- If you are using thin cotton fabric iron on the woven interfacing first. Tack (baste) around the edge of the circle of lining fabric, ¼in from the edge. You can do this on your machine using stitch length 6. Tack (baste) round the circle a second time, this time about ½in from the edge. To gather, pull both threads together (the shuttle threads if you used a machine). Lay these parts aside while you sew the edging for the bag.
- If you are using thin cotton fabric iron on the woven interfacing first. With right sides facing, sew the edge fabric together across the short sides. Fold the circular strip in four and mark the quarters on the edge to be sewn to the bag.
- Pull the basting thread on the circular piece until the bag edge is the same length as the top edge. Distribute the gathers evenly so that the marks on the circle match those on the edge. With right sides facing, pin together, preferably very closely, as this will make the sewing easier.
- Sew the parts together with a ¼in seam allowance, and then again with a ½in seam allowance.
- If the gathering thread is visible from the right side, remove it.
- Press the edging up and machine a line of stitches ¼in from the seam to make the top edge lie neatly over the gathers.

3 Assembling the lining of the bag

- Follow the same procedure as for the bag, Step 2.

4 Shoulder strap

- If you want the binding to run round the whole strap, you will need to join fabric lengths first. See 'Cutting and assembly of diagonal binding' on page 14. If you want binding on one side of the strap, you need one strip cut to the full width of the fabric.
- With right sides facing lay the strip along one edge of the strap. Start sewing the pieces together at one end and stop ³⁄₈in from the other end.

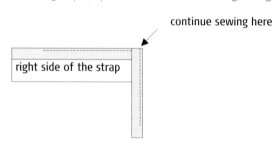

start sewing here

right side of the strap

Right side of the strap

- Fold the binding strip away from the corner at a 45 degree angle.

continue sewing here

right side of the strap

- Then fold the strip down again so that it lies along the short edge of the strap. Start the stitching as shown in the diagram and repeat at the next corner (continue down the strap if you are binding the other long edge). Finish off the seam and cut off any surplus binding. The end of the strap without binding will be hidden in the seam when you sew the lining and the outside fabric together.
- Fold the binding over to the wrong side of the strap and sew it down by hand using invisible stitches.
- To adjust the length of the strap, sew a row of buttonholes along from the bound edge. Mark along the centre of the strap with chalk or fabric marker. Measure the diameter of the button you intend to use and stitch a buttonhole following the instructions given with your machine. Continue sewing the buttonholes in a row along the marked line, spacing them evenly. Finally, slit open all the buttonholes.

5 Assembling the lining and bag fabric

- Mark the opposite sides of the bag on the upper edges of the lining and outer fabric.
- With the outer fabric of the bag right side out, pin the end of the strap without binding to one of the side edge marks, aligning the raw edges. Tack (baste) the strap in place.
- Turn the lining with the wrong side out and pull the lining over the outer fabric so that they are right sides together, matching side markings and sandwiching the end of the strap.
- Sew around the whole edge, leaving a 6in gap for turning the bag inside out.
- Tack (baste) over this opening. Press the seam allowances open across the tacked (basted) opening and then remove the tacking (basting) thread. This will produce straight edges which will be easy to sew up neatly by hand later.

- Turn the bag through the opening.
- Sew up the opening by hand using invisible stitching.
- Iron the top edges, using a cloth under the iron to prevent damage to the fabric.
- Sew two rows of stitches along the upper edge of the bag, ¼in and ½in from the edge.
- Sew buttons to the side of the bag, spacing them to match the buttonholes, and button on the free end of the strap.

6 Press stud

If you want to adjust the size of the large bag, you can fix a press stud to its base. Position the two parts of the press stud according to the marks you made when cutting the circle, 4in from the centre. Stitch through both the outer fabric and the lining.

Just Like Old Times

DESIGNED BY: Rie Norum
MACHINE QUILTED BY: Rie Norum
FINISHED QUILT SIZE: 46 × 75in
FINISHED BLOCK SIZE: Four drop block, 6in square

For a long time I have wanted to make a quilt with an antique appearance. When this block first saw the light of day on my drawing table, the time had finally come. The reproduction and Japanese fabrics were all found in cupboards, bags and forgotten project boxes. The reproduction fabrics are reprints of patterns from the period I wanted to copy, and the Japanese fabrics were added to give a worn and washed-out impression. This quilt has already fooled a couple of quilters into believing they had a genuine antique in their hands, and that sort of compliment warms the heart of a dedicated quilter. The woollen batting is especially cosy when the winter evenings are cold.

The blocks were sewn by machine and give a good effect of depth. The whole quilt is machine quilted using silk thread in various shades. If you prefer, there is no reason why you shouldn't sew this by hand using appliqué or reverse appliqué. Or perhaps a combination of hand sewing and machine sewing would suit you best?

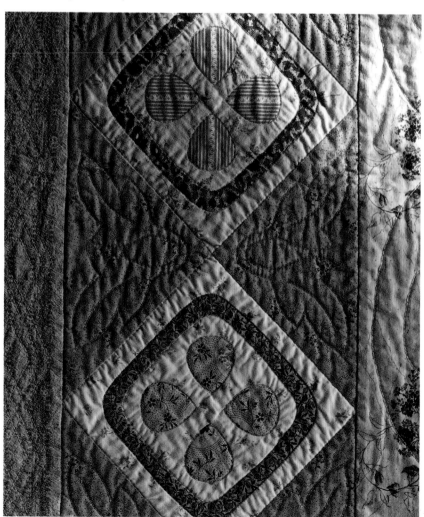

List of materials

Fabric for the four drop blocks

- 21 pieces, 7in square, for the outer background fabric
- 21 pieces, 5in square, for the inner background fabric
- 21 pieces, 5in square, for the four drop motif
- 21 pieces, 6in square, for the ring motif around the drops

Fabric for side and corner triangles, sashings and border

- 34in of fabric for the side and corner triangles
- 10in of fabric for the vertical sashing if you join the fabric, or a total length of 61in
- 77in of fabric for the outer border if the pattern is not one way and 95in if it is one way (as is the border in this design)

About 16in of fabric for binding
Fabric for backing
Cotton batting

Spray adhesive
Glue stick
About 40in of freezer paper

Cutting and assembly instructions
Four drop block

The template for the block is on page 111.

1 Cutting

- 1 piece, 7in square, for the background fabric (a).
- 1 piece, 6in square, for the ring motif (b).
- 1 piece, 5in square, for the inner background fabric (c).
- 1 piece, 5in square, for the four drops motif (d).
- The block will measure 6½in square when finished and trimmed.

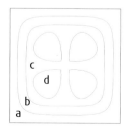

2 Assembly

- This block is sewn using the Reverse appliqué by machine technique described on page 10. To get used to the technique it is a good idea to sew some trial blocks first; the blocks for 'Dressed for the Party' on page 98 are just the thing.
- Use the template to draw two complete blocks on freezer paper. Remember to draw the outlines of the drops. On one cut out around outline 1 and on the other cut out around outline 2. Cut out the drops in the centre part which is left after cutting round outline 2 (Part 3).

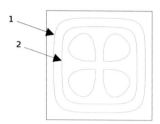

- Prepare square (a), iron on freezer paper cut according to outline 1 (see diagram below). Do the same with square (b), but iron on the freezer paper cut out around outline 2. Follow the same procedure as on page 10, starting outermost and working inwards. Glue Part 1 to Part 2. Remember: Don't begin to sew until you have glued all the parts together. Iron on to square (c) the freezer paper which was left after cutting round outline 2 (Part 3). Glue Part 2 to Part 3 and then glue this assembly to pieces (d).

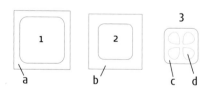

- Now you are ready to assemble the block, sewing along the outlines marked earlier.
- Sew a total of 21 blocks. Trim the blocks to 6½in square.

Side and corner triangles and sashing

1 Cutting

- 9 pieces, 9¾in square, cut diagonally to make 36 side triangles (e). If the fabric has a one-way pattern, you must take this into account when cutting.
- 6 pieces, 5¼in square, cut diagonally to make 12 corner triangles (f).
- 2 strips, 3 × 60in, for the sashing (g). If your fabric isn't long enough you will need to cut several strips and join them.

2 Assembly

- Sew two side triangles (e) to each side of a block, as shown in the diagram below.

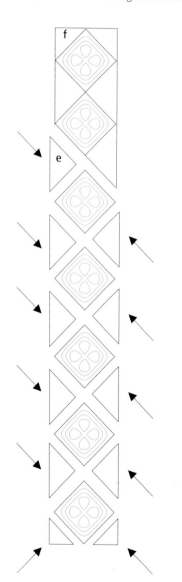

- Corner triangles (f) are attached at the top and bottom of each row of blocks.
- Sew three strips like this.
- Trim the rows of blocks to 9 × 60in.
- Sew sashing (g) between the rows of blocks.
- Trim to 31 × 60in.

Outer border

1 Cutting

- 2 pieces, 8 × 31in, of the horizontal border fabric (h).
- 2 pieces, 8 × 75in, of the vertical border fabric (i).

2 Assembly

- Sew the two horizontal borders (h) to the top and bottom of the quilt.
- Sew the two vertical borders (i) to the sides of the quilt.
- Trim to 46 × 75in. (You could leave the trimming until you have finished quilting and are ready to attach the binding.)

Quilting

The quilt is machine quilted with silk thread using stitch in the ditch on all of the seams, including those within the blocks. The quilt pattern used in the borders is a wide rope pattern, which is drawn on and then quilted.

Binding

For the binding you need a strip 210in long. The method is described in Techniques on pages 14 and 15.

g

g

i

h

Princesses Have Fun

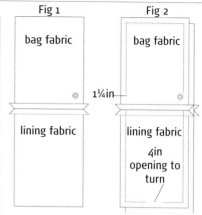

Fig 1
bag fabric
lining fabric

Fig 2
bag fabric
1¼in
lining fabric
4in opening to turn

DESIGNED BY: Unni Gullvåg / Hilde Aanerud Krohg
SEWN BY: Rie and Margrethe Norum
FINISHED SACK DIMENSIONS: 87 × 51in
FINISHED BAG DIMENSIONS: 16 × 14in

When you have daughters of a certain age, everything has to be pink. Princess dresses, crowns, tiaras, shoes and bags are important accessories. The problem is that these things are left all over the pink room and if a shoe goes missing, it's an emergency! To reduce the number of searches we have sewn sacks to store all the finery and bags, which they can use for decoration. As well as keeping all the equipment together, it is easier to remember everything that's needed when going visiting. That's when our princesses really have fun!

1 Appliqué the crown on the right side of one of the bag sack's external sides using fine zigzag stitching.

2 Sew buttons to the points of the crown.

3 Sew a bag and lining piece, right sides facing, along the top (Fig 1).

4 Iron the seam allowance towards the lining.

5 Attach an eyelet 2in below the seam on the bag piece.

6 Do the same with the other bag and lining piece. Place the pieces right sides facing, pin and sew as in Fig 2, leaving a 4in opening in the bottom of the lining.

7 Trim the seam allowances all round except for along the opening edge. Turn the sack through the opening leaving 1¼in of the lining showing at the top of the bag. Sew up the opening by hand. Iron the sack and sew two seams around the top to form a channel for the tape, starting and ending at the eyelets.

8 Attach an eyelet at the bottom of the sack, through all the layers, on the same edge as the two eyelets at the top.

9 Fold, iron and sew the tape. Use a safety pin to thread the tape through the top channel, pass one end through the lower eyelet and tie the ends together.

Princess sacks
Cutting and assembly instructions
List of materials

- 2 bag pieces, 17 × 20in, pale pink linen
- 2 lining pieces, 17 × 21in, orange fabric
- Decorations and tape
- Three orange mother-of-pearl buttons

- Princess crown appliqué, 5in square, in a golden-orange check fabric
- Three eyelets, ½in diameter
- 2in wide fabric for strap. Adjust the length to suit the girl.

Fig 3

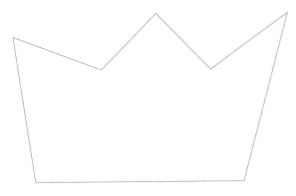

Princess bags

These are sewn in the same way as the sack, but with a small strap and no channel and eyelets. One of the bags has lining fabric which is visible at the top, while the other doesn't.

Cutting and assembly instructions

List of materials
- 2 bag pieces, 6¼ × 5½in, pale pink linen fabric
- 2 lining pieces, 6¼ × 5½in, orange fabric
- Princess crown appliqué, 5in square, in a golden-orange check fabric
- Three orange mother-of-pearl buttons
- 2in wide fabric for strap. Adjust the length to suit the girl.

1 Appliqué the crown on the right side of one of the bag's sides using fine zigzag stitching.
2 Sew buttons to the points on the crown.
3 Sew bag and lining, right sides facing, along one long side (see Fig 1).
4 Iron the seam allowance against the lining.
5 Do the same with the other bag and lining piece. Place the pieces, right sides facing, pin and sew all round as in Fig 2, leaving a 2½in opening in the lining.
6 Trim the seam allowance all round except for along the opening. Turn the bag through the opening. Sew up the opening by hand.
7 Fold up the lining if you want a little of it to show at the top (see Fig 3) or push the whole of the lining into the bag. Iron and stitch in the ditch along the seam if the lining is showing.
8 Fold in ½in along both long sides of the strap strip and press. Fold in half lengthways, with wrong sides facing, iron and then stitch along each side of the strap ⅛in from the edges. Turn in the ends and stitch across.
9 Sew a button at each side of the bag and a buttonhole each end of thestrap. Button the strap on the bag.

Fig 3

Fig 1

bag fabric
lining fabric

Fig 2

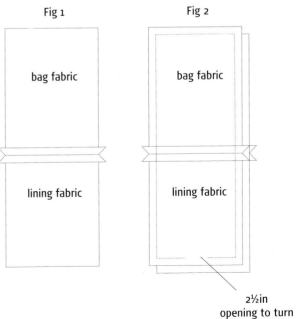

bag fabric
lining fabric

2½in
opening to turn

Sitting Pretty

DESIGNED BY: Rie Norum
SEWN BY: Rie Norum

It is Bruin's birthday and time for a party! There have to be extra things to sit on, too, in all sorts of shapes.

The word pouffe has always fascinated me, and I can use it as often as I like since these were added to the kids' room.

List of materials

The pouffes are filled with Styrofoam beads, which can be bought in various sizes from craft shops.

Round pouffe
- About 27½in of fabric for sides, top and base
- About 12in of fabric for piping
- About 85in of ¼in diameter cotton cord
- One 12in zip fastener
- About 27½in of iron-on woven interfacing for reinforcement if you are using thin cotton fabric
- About 14in of batting with an iron-on side for the top

Square pouffe
- About 27½in of fabric for four sides
- About 14in of fabric for top, base and handles
- About 12in of fabric for piping
- About 157½in of ¼in diameter cotton cord
- One 12in zip fastener
- About 41½in of iron-on woven interfacing for reinforcement if you are using thin cotton fabric
- About 14in of thin batting with an iron-on side for the top
- 4 buttons

Pyramid-shaped pouffe
- About 49in of fabric for four sides, top and base
- About 12in of fabric for handles and piping
- About 167in of ¼in diameter cotton cord
- One 16in zip fastener
- About 49in of iron-on woven interfacing for reinforcement if you are using thin cotton fabric
- About 14in of thin batting with an iron-on side for the top
- 2 buttons

Single edge cord foot to sew on the piping – you can also use a zipper foot.

Round pouffe

1 Cutting the top, sides, base and edge cord
- Cut 16 pieces, 3½in square, for the top (a).
- Cut a piece, 12½ × 38in, for the sides (b).

a

b

- Cut two pieces, 8 × 12½in, for the base (c).

c

- Cut 1in strips at 45 degrees to the fabric weave, as shown in the diagram. Cut enough to make a strip 84in long after joining them together. If you have 12in of fabric you will need 6 strips.

2 Preparing the top
- Sew together the 16 squares of the top (a) in four rows of four blocks.

x4

- Iron the seam allowances in alternating directions and then sew the four rows together.

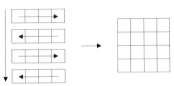

- Place the iron-on side of the thin batting on the wrong side of the top. Iron in place, using a cloth under the iron to protect it.
- Quilt the top piece using a pattern of your choice.
- Draw a 12½in diameter circle on the top. Either draw the circle directly on the fabric, using a pair of compasses set at 6¼in and with the point at the centre, or make a paper pattern. The measurement includes the seam allowance. Cut out.

3 Prepare the piping as described on Page

11.

4 Preparing the sides
- Iron the woven interfacing on to the wrong side of the side fabric (b) if you are using a thin cotton. For thicker fabrics, the stiffening is not needed.
- Fold the side fabric (b) in half with the short edges matching and right sides facing. Sew a seam ¼in from the edge. Press the seam allowances open.
- Pin the piping to the right side of the side piece along one long edge so that the seam allowances match the edge of the side piece. Sew the piping all the way round, continuing so that the ends overlap. See the instructions on page 11.

5 Preparing the base
- Iron woven interfacing on to the wrong side of the two rectangles for the base (c) if you are using a thin cotton. For thicker fabrics, stiffening is not needed.
- Sew the zip fastener to the long edges of the two rectangles as described in Zip fasteners on page 11.
- Cut the base into a circle in the same way as the top.

6 Assembling the top, sides and base

- Divide the top piece into 4 equal parts and mark with pins. Do the same with the base piece and both long edges of the side piece. With right sides facing, pin the top piece to the long edge of the side piece with the piping. The piping will now be sandwiched between the layers of fabric. Make sure that the marks on each part coincide exactly. Sew a seam around the edge, slightly inside the previous seam and closer to the piping.
- Attach the base piece to the other long side edge in the same way, remembering to open the zip fastener before pinning on the bottom.

- Place the iron-on side of the thin batting on the wrong side of the top. Iron in place, using a cloth under the iron to protect it.
- Quilt the top piece using a pattern of your choice.

3 Prepare the piping as described on page 11.

- The piping is sewn on to the right side of the top piece. Starting at the centre of one of the sides, pin the piping so that the seam allowances match the edges of the top piece. You will need to snip into the seam allowance in order to turn the corners. Sew all the way round, continuing so that the ends overlap. See the instructions on page 11.

4 Preparing the sides

- Iron woven interfacing on to the wrong side of the side fabric (b) if you are using a thin cotton. For thicker fabrics, stiffening is not needed.
- The piping is sewn on to the right side of one edge of each side piece. Pin the piping so that the seam allowances match the edge of the side piece and cut off. Pull the cord slightly at each end and cut it obliquely. This prevents lumps at the corners when the top and base are sewn on.

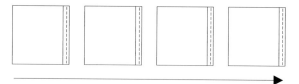

- Sew the piping in place just within the seam you made when preparing it.
- Trim off the ends if they stick out at each end.
- With right sides facing, sandwiching the piping, sew the four sides together, using four seams in all, to produce a tube.

5 Preparing the base

- Iron woven interfacing on to the wrong side of the two base rectangles (c) if using thin cotton. For thicker fabrics, stiffening is not needed.
- Sew the zip fastener to the two rectangles (c) as described in Zip fasteners on page 11.
- Trim the base to 12½in square.
- Add piping in the same way as for the top in Step 3.

6 Assembling the top, sides and base

- With right sides facing, pin the top piece to the side piece matching side seams to corners and sandwiching the piping round the top. To turn the corners, cut a slit through all the layers of fabric, almost reaching the seam. Sew each side separately, starting and stopping ¼in from the edges. The seam should be just inside the previous seam and slightly closer to the piping. Repeat for the remaining three sides.
- Do the same with the base piece, but remember to open the zip fastener before pinning it on.

Square pouffe

1 Cutting the top, sides, base and piping

- Cut 4 pieces, 6½in square, for the top (a).

 a

- Cut 4 pieces, 12½in square, for the sides (b).

 b

- Cut 2 pieces, 8 × 12½in, for the base (c).

c

- Cut 2 pieces, 2 × 10in, for the handles (d).

 d

- Cut 1in strips at 45 degrees to the weave, as shown opposite, for piping. Cut enough to make a strip 157in long after joining them. If you have 12in of fabric you will need 11 strips.

2 Preparing the top piece

- Sew together the four squares (a) in pairs for the top piece.

- Sew together the two pairs after ironing the seam allowances in alternating directions, as shown in the diagram, to make a four-patch block:

Pyramid-shaped pouffe

1 Cutting the top, sides, base and piping

- Cut one piece, 12in square, for the top (a).

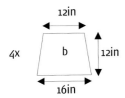

- Cut four sides to the measurements below (b).

- Cut two pieces, 10 × 16in, for the base (c).

c

- Cut 2 pieces, 2 × 10in, for the handles (d).

d

- Cut 1in strips at 45 degrees to the fabric weave as shown below for piping. Cut enough to make a strip 157in long when joined together. If you have 12in of fabric you will need 11 strips.

2 Preparing the top

- Iron woven interfacing on to the wrong side of the top fabric (a) if using thin cotton. For thicker fabrics, stiffening is not needed.

3 Prepare the piping as described on page 11

- Add piping to the top in the same way as in Step 3 of the square pouffe.

4 Preparing the handles and sides

- Iron woven interfacing on to the wrong side of the side pieces (b) if using thin cotton. For thicker fabrics, stiffening is not needed.
- Sew on the handles before assembling the sides. Fold the fabric for the handle in half, right sides facing, and starting at the folded edge, sew a seam around the edge leaving an opening on the long edge. Cut off the corners before turning to the right side.

- Iron the seams and use invisible stitches to sew up the turning

opening by hand. Machine stitch round the whole strip, ¼in from the edge.

- The piping is sewn on to the right side of one edge of each side piece. Pin the piping so that the seam allowances match the edge of the side piece and cut off. Pull the cord slightly at each end and cut it obliquely. This prevents lumps at the corners when the top and base are sewn on.
- Sew the piping in place, just within the seam you made when preparing it.
- Trim off the ends if they stick out at each end.
- With right sides facing, sandwiching the piping, sew the four sides

together, using four seams in all, to produce a tube.

5 Preparing the base

- Iron woven interfacing on to the wrong side of the two base rectangles (c) if using thin cotton. For thicker fabrics, stiffening is not needed.
- Sew the zip fastener to the two rectangles (c) as described in Zip fasteners on page 11.
- Trim the base to 16in square.
- Add piping in the same way as for the top in Step 3 of the square pouffe.

6 Assembling the top, sides and base

- With right sides facing, pin the top piece to the side piece matching side seams to corners and sandwiching the piping round the top. To turn the corners, cut a slit through all the layers of fabric, almost reaching the seam. Sew each side separately, starting and stopping ¼in from the edges. The seam should be just inside the previous seam and slightly closer to the piping. Repeat for the remaining three sides.
- Do the same with the base piece, but remember to open the zip fastener before pinning it on.

Sweet Dreams

DESIGNED BY: Rie Norum
MACHINE QUILTED BY: Rie Norum
FINISHED QUILT SIZE: 47³/₈ × 72⁷/₈in
FINISHED BLOCK SIZE: Walter's Place block, 6³/₈in square

Every princess needs her own quilt. It should glitter and shine and brighten up the rainiest of days. If you know the magic spell, perhaps it will even take off and carry you away to the ends of the earth …

This quilt is sprinkled with sequins and mother-of-pearl buttons. The sequins were sewn on by hand, one by one, using backstitching. The block is called Walter's Place and I had so much fun sewing it that I made enough blocks for two quilts!

List of materials

Fabric for Walter's Place blocks
- 23 pieces, 10 × 12in, background fabrics
- 23 pieces, 10 × 12in, of floral fabrics

Fabric for the four-patch blocks and border
- About 34in of striped shirting fabric for four-patch blocks
- About 77in of fabric, if it does not have a one-way pattern, or 95in if it does, as in the trellis floral border used here

About 16in of fabric for binding
Fabric for backing
Cotton batting

Cutting and assembly instructions
Walter's Place block
Cut and sew 23 blocks.

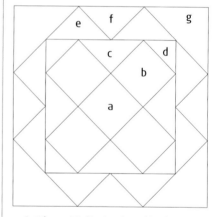

1 Cutting a Walter's Place block
- 1 piece, 2in square, of the floral fabric (a).
- 4 pieces, 2in square, of the background fabric (b).
- 1 piece, 3½in square, of floral fabric cut diagonally to make 4 triangles (c).
- 2 pieces, 2¼in square, of floral fabric cut diagonally to make 4 triangles (d).
- 2 pieces, 3¾in square, of floral fabric cut diagonally to make 8 triangles (e).
- 1 piece, 3¾in square, of background fabric cut diagonally to make 4 triangles (f).
- 2 pieces, 3¼in square, of background fabric cut diagonally to make 4 triangles (g).
- The block will measure 6⅞in square when finished and trimmed.

2 Assembling the Walter's Place block

- Start by sewing together the central section of the block.
- First sew together (b) + (a) + (b).
- Sew (c) + (b) + (c), twice and sew one of these on each side of the (b) + (a) + (b) strip.
- Finally, sew on the four corner triangles (d).
- Trim the block to 4¾in square.

- Now make the outer edges by sewing together (e) + (f) + (e). Sew a total of 4 outer edges of this type.
  Note: you must use a seam allowance of ³⁄₈in, which can be done by using the ordinary pressure foot on your machine.

- Trim the lower edge of the block to ¼in from where the seams meet at the 'tip'.
- Sew the outer edges (e) + (f) + (e) to the central section of the block.

- Finally, sew on the four corner triangles (g).

- Trim the block to 6⅞in square.
- Sew 23 blocks.

Four-patch block

1 Cutting the block

4 pieces, 3¾in square, of striped shirting fabric (h).

2 Assembling the block

Sew together the squares (h) to make a four-patch block (see page 7). If using striped fabric alternate the direction of the blocks (see diagram). The block will measure 6⅞in square when finished and trimmed.

Make 22 blocks.

Border and assembling the quilt

Cutting the border

- 2 pieces, 7¾ × 47⅞in, of floral trellis fabric (i).
- 2 pieces, 7¾ × 57⅞in, of floral trellis fabric (j).

2 Assembling the central section and outer border

- Sew together the Walter's Place blocks and four-patch blocks in rows as shown in the diagram.
- The central section will measure 32⅜ × 57⅞in.
- Sew the two long borders (i) to the sides of the quilt.
- Sew the two short borders (j) to the top and bottom of the quilt.
- Trim to 47⅜ × 72⅞in. (You could leave the trimming until you have finished quilting and are ready to attach the binding.)

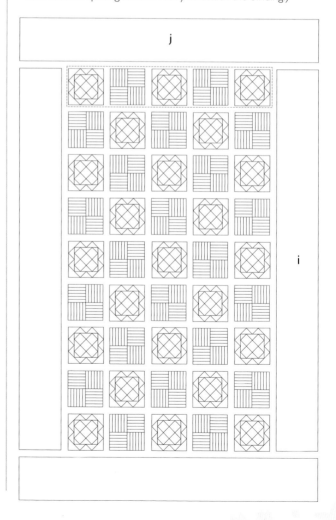

Quilting
The centre of the quilt is machine quilted with silk thread using stitch in the ditch, in all seams including those within the blocks. A scalloped pattern with corner motifs is used for the quilting pattern in the border.

Binding
For the binding you need a strip 255in long. The method is described in Techniques on pages 14 and 15.

Buttons and sequins
If you want to add buttons and sequins, you should sew them on after it has been washed. The sequins (about 4000 of them) are sewn on by hand using backstitching along the quilting pattern.

For a Little Gentleman

DESIGNED BY: Rie Norum
MACHINE QUILTED BY: Rie Norum
FINISHED QUILT SIZE: 39¾ × 72¾in
FINISHED BLOCK SIZE: Walter's Place block, 6⅞in square

I usually have a couple of blocks left over after every sewing project, but after the 'Sweet Dreams' quilt there were so many that I had enough for a whole new quilt. Since the first was very feminine I wanted the next quilt to suit a little boy. I chose sashing instead of filler squares to provide variation in the quilts, each of which will be in its own child's bedroom.

List of materials

Fabric for the Walter's Place blocks
- 21 pieces, 10 × 12in, background fabrics
- 21 pieces, 10 × 12in, of floral fabrics

Fabrics for the sashing, corner squares and border
- About 31½in of striped fabric for sashing
- About 8in of yellow floral fabric for the corner squares
- About 63in of spotted fabric for the border

About 14in of fabric for binding
Fabric for backing
Cotton batting

Cutting and assembly instructions
Walter's Place block
Cut and sew 22 blocks.

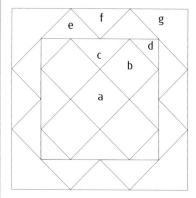

1 Cutting the Walter's Place block
Use the same method as given for the Sweet Dreams quilt on page 80.

2 Assembling the Walter's Place block
- Use the same method as for the Sweet Dreams quilt, Step 2, page 82.
- Sew 21 blocks, to make the quilt.
- Trim the blocks to 6⅞in square.

Sashing and corner squares
1 Cutting the sashing
- 52 pieces, 2½ × 6⅞in, for sashings (h).

h

- 32 pieces, 2½in square, for corner squares (i).

i

2 Assembling the sashing, corner squares and blocks

- Sew together 4 squares (i) and 3 sashings (h) to make 8 strips.

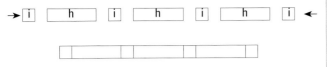

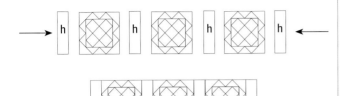

- Sew together 4 sashings (h) and 3 blocks to make 7 strips:

- Finally sew the strips together from top to bottom. Start with a row of sashing, then a row of blocks, and so on. Finish with a row of sashing, as shown in the diagram below. The central section will measure $26\frac{3}{8} \times 62\frac{7}{8}$in.

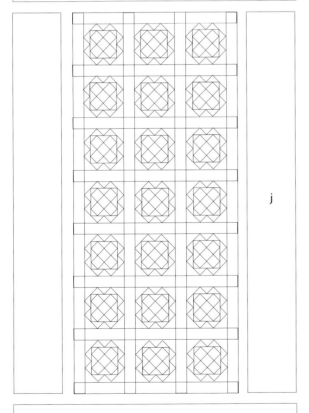

Border

1 Cutting the border

- 2 pieces, $6\frac{3}{4} \times 60\frac{1}{4}$in, of the check border fabric (j).
- 2 pieces, $6\frac{3}{4} \times 39\frac{3}{4}$in, of the check border fabric (k).

2 Assembling the border

- Sew the two long borders (j) to the sides of the quilt.
- Sew the two short borders (k) to the top and bottom of the quilt.
- Trim to $39\frac{3}{4} \times 72\frac{3}{4}$in. (You could leave the trimming until you have finished quilting and are ready to attach the binding.)

Quilting

The centre of the quilt is machine quilted with silk thread using stitch in the ditch, for all seams including those within the blocks. The border pattern in the sashing and squares is worked vertically and then filled in horizontally, and a leaf-pattern is used for the border. Draw them using a plastic template and marking chalk.

Binding

For the binding you need a strip 240in long. The method is described in Techniques on pages 14 and 15.

A Page to Colour...

DESIGNED BY: Rie Norum
MACHINE QUILTED BY: Rie Norum
FINISHED QUILT SIZE: 33½in square
FINISHED BLOCK SIZE: Pencil block, 3in square

When my youngest, Edvard Otelius was born, there was a slight change in my fabric buying habits and more masculine fabrics now became more appropriate. He needed a little crawl quilt, I thought, but before the quilt was finished he was way past the crawling stage and had become a little man who wanted to meet the world on his feet. As a result, the quilt became a comforter for his bed.

List of materials
Fabrics for pencil blocks
- 49 pieces, 3 × 3½in, of bright fabric for the pencils
- 14 pieces, 1½ × 3in, of bright fabric for the pencil points along the edge of the central section
- 49 pieces, 2 × 6in, of light shirting fabric for the background

Fabric for the border
- 10in of a muted fabric for inner border
- 22in of a floral fabric for outer border

About 10in of dark fabric for binding
Fabric for backing
Cotton batting
About 40in of freezer paper

Cutting and assembly instructions
Pencil block
The template for the block is on page 118.

1 Cutting
- Cut 1 piece, 1½ × 3½in, for the pencil (a).
- Cut 2 pieces, 1½in square, for the pencil points (b). Note: the two (b) parts are made of the same fabric as the (a) parts in adjacent blocks. It is a good idea to lay out the pieces on a design wall as you cut them out before assembly (see page 18).
- Cut 4 pieces, 1½ × 2in, for the background (c).
- The block will measure 3½in square when finished and trimmed.

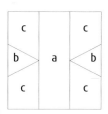

2 Assembly
- For accurate results, the pencil blocks are sewn on freezer paper without sewing through the paper.
- Draw the block on freezer paper and include the dotted line across (a), which is used when you sew the parts together. Cut along the lines between (a) and (c).

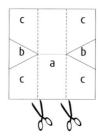

- On Units 1 and 3, fold the paper along the line between (c) and (b).

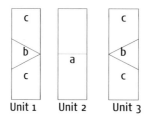

Unit 1   Unit 2   Unit 3

- Iron the freezer paper pattern (Fig 1) with the glossy side against the wrong side of the fabric for the triangle (b).
- Fold the freezer paper back (Fig 2) along the line between (b) and (c).

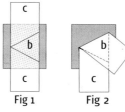

Fig 1   Fig 2

- Place the fabric for part (c) with its right side facing the fabric for part (b) and sew along the edge of the paper (Fig 3). Take care not to sew through the paper!
- Cut away the surplus seam allowance (Fig 4), open the fabric out against the freezer paper and, with seam allowances turned away from part (b), iron flat.

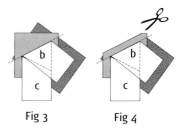

Fig 3   Fig 4

- Repeat for the remaining part (c), to complete Unit 1. Do not remove the paper until the sewing of the block is completely finished.
- Repeat the same procedure for Unit 3.
- Sew together Units 1 and 2. With right sides facing, pin them together. Make sure that the point of part (b) touches the centre of part (a), using the dotted line for reference. Again, be careful not to sew through the paper!
- Now sew Units 1 and 2 to Unit 3 as described above.
- Trim the blocks to 3½in square.
- Peel off the freezer paper.
- Sew a total of 49 blocks.

3 Assembly

- Spread the blocks out and sew them together in rows of seven. Remember to rotate the blocks 90 degrees to each other along the row, as shown in the diagram. Sew a total of seven rows of this type.

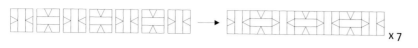 × 7

- Sew the seven rows together. Make sure the seam allowances are ironed in alternate directions before you sew the rows together, as shown in the diagram below:
- The central section should measure 21½in square.

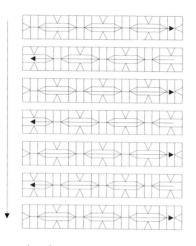 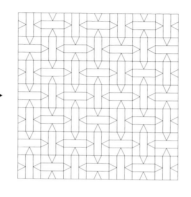

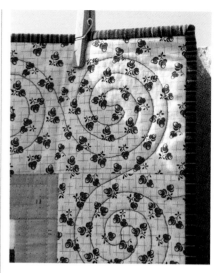

The impression this gives of being a child's quilt is further emphasised by the quilting. The flourishes in the framework definitely belong with the pencils in the centre of the quilt. Dark brown silk thread is used which provides a good contrast with the background fabric.

Inner border

1 Cutting

- Cut 2 strips, 2 × 21½in, of the inner border fabric (d).
- Cut 2 strips, 2 × 24½in, of the inner border fabric (e).

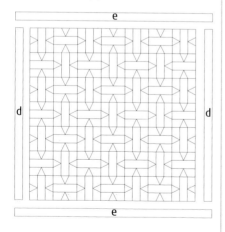

2 Assembly

- Sew the two strips (d) to the sides of the quilt.
- Sew the two strips (e) to the top and bottom of the quilt.

Outer border

1 Cutting

- 2 pieces, 5 × 24½in, of the outer border fabric (f).
- 2 pieces, 5 × 33½in, of the outer border fabric (g).

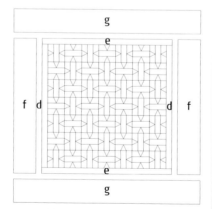

2 Assembly

- Sew the two outer borders (f) to the sides of the quilt.
- Sew the two outer borders (g) to the top and bottom of the quilt.
- Trim to 33½in square. (You could leave trimming until you have finished quilting and are ready to attach the binding.)

Quilting

The centre of the quilt is quilted using stitch in the ditch, worked by machine, using silk thread. The quilt pattern in the outer border is drawn with marking chalk using a plastic template.

Binding

For the binding you need a strip 150in long. The procedure is described in Techniques on pages 14 and 15.

If you want to conjure up an antique mood, you can replace a piece of fabric here and there to give an impression of fabric rationing.

Rie's Rag Rug

DESIGNED BY: Rie Norum
HAND QUILTED BY: Anne Fjellvær
FINISHED QUILT SIZE: 23¾ × 38in

The inspiration for this quilt was some antique Indian rugs. The Indian rugs were colourful and beautifully quilted, closely packed with thread in all the colours of the rainbow – and I really fell for the quilting. The fabrics I used are mainly muted Japanese fabrics with a few additions of reproduction fabrics. For this one I delved deep into my treasure chest – I wish it were possible to get hold of more of these fabrics. To emphasise the impression of age, a small 'repair' patch is appliquéd on before quilting.

Front piece

1 Cutting

- Cut 1 piece, 19½ × 2½in, (a).
- Cut 1 piece, 19½ × 6½in, (b).
- Cut 1 piece, 19½ × 11in, (c).
- Cut 1 piece, 19½ × 5½in, (d).
- Cut 1 piece, 6 × 5½in, (e).
- Cut 1 piece, 6 × 18½in, (f).
- Cut 1 piece, 13½ × 8½in, (g).
- Cut 1 piece, 13½ × 15½in, (h).
- Cut 1 piece, 2¾ × 4¾in, (i) (optional).

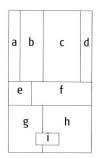

2 Assembly

- Spread out the parts in their correct positions and orientations.
- Begin by sewing together parts (a) and (b).

- Then sew together parts (c) and (d).

- Now sew together (a) + (b) and (c) + (d).

- Sew part (e) to part (f).

- Sew part (g) to part (h). A small patch (i) is appliquéd on to part (g) + (h), to give an antique appearance, but this is optional. Fold in a ¼in seam allowance on all four sides of part (i), place it where you want it and appliqué by hand using invisible stitching.

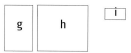

- Sew (e) + (f) to (g) + (h).

- Finally sew (a) + (b) +(c) + (d) to (e) + (f) + (g) + (h).

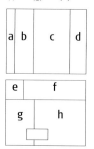

- The front should measure 23½ × 38in.

Back piece

1 Cutting

- Cut 1 piece, 15 × 11½in, (j).
- Cut 1 piece, 8½ × 11½in, (k).
- Cut 1 piece, 4½ × 11½in, (l).
- Cut 1 piece, 14½ × 11½in, (m).
- Cut 1 piece, 18 × 4in, (n).
- Cut 1 piece, 18 × 8¼in, (o).
- Cut 1 piece, 6 × 17in, (p).
- Cut 1 piece, 6 × 7in, (q).
- Cut 1 piece, 4 × 2in, (r).
- Cut 1 piece, 4 × 22in, (s).

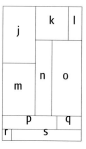

2 Assembly

- Spread out the parts in their correct positions and orientations.
- Begin by sewing together parts (k) and (l).

- Then sew together parts (n) and (o).

- Now sew together (k) + (l) and (n) + (o).

- Sew part (j) to part (m).

- Sew these to parts (k) + (l) + (n) + (o).

- Sew together part (p) and part (q).

- Sew together part (r) and part (s).

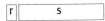

- Now sew (p) + (q) to (r) + (s).

- Finally sew (p) + (q) + (r) + (s) to (j) + (k) + (l) + (m) + (n) + (o).

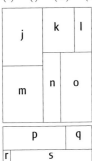

- The back should measure 23½ × 38in.

Assembly

The quilt is sewn inside out.

- Begin by laying the back piece with its wrong side against the batting. Tack (baste) all the way round using a ¼in seam allowance.
- Trim off any surplus batting which extends beyond the seam, cutting as close to the seam as you can.
- Now place the back piece and front piece, right sides facing, and sew all round using a ¼in seam allowance. Leave a 6in opening for turning the quilt later.
- Tack (baste) across the opening. Iron the seam allowances open all the way round the quilt and then remove the tacking (basting) thread. This will produce a neat, straight edge to the opening which will make it easier to sew it up by hand later.
- Cut off the corners diagonally, close to the seam.

The quilt is edged with colourful tassels. The inspiration was Indian, but the result has more of a Japanese character. The quilting is done in stripes with ¼in spacing, both horizontally and vertically, even diagonally, along the length of the quilt. Because of the closely spaced quilting, the quilt shrank appreciably, even before washing! The tassels were added after the quilt had been shrunk completely in the washing machine set on delicate wash.

- Turn the quilt through the opening, taking care to get the corners sharp. Iron the quilt to make the edges flat, preferably using a cloth under the iron to prevent damage to the fabric.
- Sew up the opening by hand using invisible stitching. The quilt should now measure 23 × 37½in.
- Baste the quilt together and begin quilting.
- You can spray-baste the back piece to the batting before tacking (basting) them together along the outer edge (see Assembly, first step). If you want to spray-baste the back to the front, you must do this after turning the quilt and before you sew up the opening.

Quilting

This rug is quilted by hand using silk thread in various colours to match the fabrics. The quilting is done in parallel lines, ¼in apart. The direction of the quilting is indicated by pink lines in the diagram below. Wash the quilt before attaching the tassels.

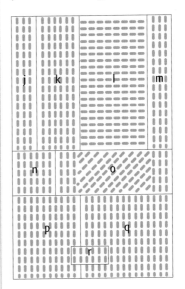

Tassels

To give the quilt an oriental appearance I added tassels sewn along the short end edges. The tassels are made of mouliné yarn wound round a dowel with a diameter of about 1¼in. When you feel the tassel is thick enough, remove the yarn from the rod, tie the loop together and then wind the end of the yarn round the top and secure it before sewing the tassel to the quilt. Finally, trim the ends of the tassels, making sure they are all the same length.

Green Tweed Handbag

DESIGNED BY: Rie Norum
SEWN BY: Rie Norum

How many handbags does one need? One for every occasion is probably the only answer. Make a smart tweed version or add sequins to a floral fabric as shown opposite.

List of materials

- About 10in of tweed fabric for the bag fronts
- About 10in of cotton fabric for the sides and base
- About 12in of fabric for the lining and pocket if required
- About 10in of iron-on interfacing
- About 10in of batting, with or without an adhesive side
- Handles
- Plastic template sheet for base

The templates for the pattern are on pages 108 and 109.

Cutting and assembly instructions

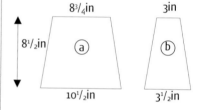

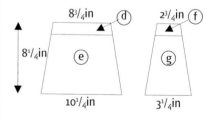

Outer pieces and lining

1 Cutting the outer pieces, lining and pocket

- Cut out two bag fronts (a) in tweed fabric. Cut out iron-on batting the same size and iron on to the wrong side of the fabric.
- Cut out two side pieces (b) in cotton fabric. Cut out iron-on batting the same size and iron on to the wrong side of the fabric.
- Cut out two base pieces (c) in cotton fabric. Cut out iron-on batting the same size and iron on to the wrong side of the fabric.
- Cut out two front lining edges (d), 2 × 10¼in, in cotton fabric.
- Cut out two front lining pieces (e), 6¾ × 10¼in, in cotton fabric.
- Cut out two side lining edges (f), 2 × 3¼in, for the side pieces in cotton fabric.
- Cut out two side lining pieces (g), 6¾ × 3¼in, for the side pieces in cotton fabric.
- Cut out a base for the lining (h) in cotton fabric.
- Cut out an additional base for the lining, 3½ × 9¾in, from leftover fabric, to use as a pocket for the base plate.
- Cut out two pieces of interfacing for the fronts of the lining fabric (a).
- Cut out two pieces of interfacing for the sides of the lining fabric (b).
- If you want a pocket in the bag, cut a rectangle, 3½ × 8½in, and interfacing 3 × 8in. The size of the pocket can be varied to suit your own requirements.
- Cut out two base plates from plastic template sheet (i).

2 Assembling the pocket

- Centre the interfacing and iron on to the wrong side of the fabric.
- Fold the interfaced fabric in half, right sides facing, and sew the side and bottom edges together using a ¼in seam allowance. Leave an opening of about an inch at the bottom to turn through.

- Cut off the corners to within 2–3 threads of the seam. Turn the pocket inside out. Iron.
- If you want to add stitching along the top edge of the pocket, sew this now, about ¼in from the edge.

3 Assembling the lining

- Sew together the top piece (d) and the bottom (e) parts of the lining. Iron the seam allowances open. Repeat for the other two lining pieces.
- Iron interfacing on to the wrong side of the two lining pieces.
- If you want a pocket in the bag, you should sew it on now. Place the pocket on the right side of one of the lining pieces and sew along the sides and bottom edges.
- Sew together the top (f) and the bottom (g) parts of the side lining. Iron the seams open. Repeat for the other two side lining pieces.
- Iron interfacing on to the wrong side of the two pieces of lining for the sides.
- Sew lining pieces (d) + (e) to side pieces (f) + (g).
- Repeat for the other two lining pieces.
- Sew pieces (d) + (e) + (f) + (g) to (d) + (e) + (f) + (g). Leave a 4in opening on one side of the lining pieces to turn through.
- Iron the seams open.
- Place the 3½ × 9¾in piece of leftover fabric, against the wrong side of the lining fabric base piece, (h). This will create a pocket into which the plastic sheet fits.
- Sew the base on to the lining of the bag, starting with sides (d) + (e). Start and finish the seam ¼in from the edges. Do the same for the side piece seams. Take care not to sew the leftover fabric all the way round as the pocket must have an opening.

4 Assembling the outer parts

- Sew the front piece (a) to a side piece (b).
- Repeat for the remaining two outer pieces.
- Sew pieces (a) + (b) to (a) + (b).
- Trim away any surplus batting from the outside of the seams and iron the seams towards the fronts of the bag.
- Sew on the base (c), starting with parts (a). Start and finish the seam ¼in from the edges. Do the same with the side seams on parts (b).

5 Assembling the bag

- Turn the bag so that the wrong side is facing out.
- Place the lining fabric in the bag so that the the the right sides are facing.
- Place the handles between the lining and outer fabric with the ends sticking out of the bag. Sew together using a ¼in seam allowance. It is wise here to tack (baste) the parts together first and check that the handles are located correctly.
- Turn the bag through the opening in the lining. Push the plastic base through the opening in the lining fabric into the pocket in the base of the bag. Trim it if necessary to fit the pocket
- Sew up the opening in the lining fabric by hand using invisible stitching.
- Sew stitching along the top edge of the bag, about ¼in from the edge.
- Iron the bag, using a cloth under the iron to protect the fabric.

Brown Tweed Bag

DESIGNED BY: Rie Norum
SEWN BY: Rie Norum

This design was also sewn from tweed fabric, but you can use any other kind of fabric as shown in the picture opposite.

List of materials
- About 16in of tweed fabric
- About 12in of fabric for the lining and pocket if required
- About 16in of iron-on interfacing
- About 16in of iron-on woven interfacing
- About 6in of fabric for handle
- About 45in of thick cord for the handle
- Plastic template sheet for the base

The template for the pattern is on page 110. Enlarge the pieces by 200 per cent to 12½ × 15½in.

Cutting and assembly instructions

Outer pieces and lining

1 Cutting the outer pieces, lining and pocket
- Cut two bag fronts, 13¼ × 16in, and two top parts of the lining for the inside of the bag, 4¼ × 16in, in your chosen fabric. This includes a seam allowance of ¼in.
- Cut out two pieces of woven interfacing the same size as the bag and iron on to the wrong side of the fabric.
- Cut out two bottom pieces of lining, 9½ × 16in in your chosen fabric and a piece of interfacing the same size, which is ironed on to the wrong side of the fabric.
- If you want a pocket in the bag, cut a piece of lining fabric, 3½ × 8½in, and a piece of interfacing 3 × 8in. The size of the pocket can be varied to suit your own requirements.

2 Assembling the pocket
- Centre the interfacing and iron on to the wrong side of the pocket fabric.
- Fold in half, right sides facing and sew the side and bottom edges together using a ¼in seam. Leave an opening of about an inch at the bottom for turning through.
- Cut off the corners to within 2-3 threads of the seam and turn the pocket inside out. Iron.
- If you want to add stitching about ¼in from the top edge, do this now.

3 Assembling the lining
- Sew together the top and bottom parts of the lining. Iron the seam allowance against the lining.
- If you have made a pocket place it on one of the lining pieces as shown on the template and sew along the side and bottom edges.

4 Assembling the bag
- Lay the bag front on the lining fabric, right sides facing, and sew along the curved upper edge of the bag. Cut slits in the seam allowance to within 2–3 threads of the seam and about ½in apart. Sew across the top edge of the bag, starting 1in from the curved seam, to the sides.

- Repeat for the remaining two pieces.
- Turn the parts to the right side and iron. Topstitch round the curve, 1in from the edge (see Stitching 1 on template). A simple way to do this is to draw the part on freezer paper, iron it along the edge of the curve and sew along the outer edge of the freezer paper. Repeat for the other side.

- Now sew the bag together at the sides. Place the two parts, right sides facing, with lining fabric against lining fabric and bag front against bag front. Pin and sew the sides together leaving a 4in opening on one side of the lining pieces to turn through, as shown on the template. Trim any surplus stiffening along the outside of the seam.
- Press the seams apart and sew the base of the lining and the front piece together.
- Fold each corner so that the base seam and side seam match and the fabrics form a triangle. Sew a seam measuring 3½in long straight across the corner, as in the diagram below.

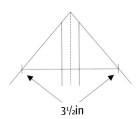

3½in

- Cut off the corner and zigzag stitch along the cut edge.
- Repeat for the other three corners.
- Turn the bag through the opening left in the lining.
- If you want to put a base in the bag, you should do so now. Sew stitching from corner to corner along the front and back edges of the bag, sewing through both outer fabric and lining. This will create a pocket in the base of the bag measuring 3½ × 12in. Cut a piece of stiff plastic sheet, about 3¼ × 11¾in, and push it through the opening in the lining fabric into the pocket. Trim to fit.
- Sew up the opening in the lining fabric by hand using invisible stitching.

This blue and brown handbag is sewn in the same way as the brown tweed bag. Notice what a different impression the bag gives with different fabric.

- Topstitch along the upper edge of the bag 1in from the edge (see Stitching 2 on the template). Sew from the curve on one bag front to the curve on the other. Repeat with the other side.

The handle for the bag
1 Cutting
- Cut two strips of fabric, 2 × 21½in.
- Cut two cords, 22in long.

2 Assembly
- Fold one fabric strip, right sides facing, and sew together with a ¼in seam. Repeat with the other strip. Press the seam open.
- Pin one end of the cord with a safety pin to one end of the strip of fabric and turn the fabric strip to the right side. This way, you turn the strip at the same time as threading the cord through. Keep the seam allowances open when turning, to avoid any lumps. Repeat with the other handle.

- Thread the handle through the curved channel along the top edge of the bag.
- Trim the ends and sew them together by hand. Secure with a few stitches to prevent the cord from moving around when you use the bag. This is important since the fabric of the handle may stretch with use if it isn't sewn securely.
- Hide the join in the handle ends by pulling the handle until it is hidden in the channel. Repeat with the other handle.

Decoration
You can add an appliqué or some kind of decoration to the bag. An appliqué must be sewn on before you begin to sew the parts together in Step 4, Assembling the bag.

Dear Hattie

DESIGNED BY: Rie Norum
MACHINE QUILTED BY: Rie Norum
FINISHED QUILT SIZE: 35⅝ × 48½in
FINISHED BLOCK SIZE: Hattie's Hen House, 4½in square

The block in this quilt is a simplified version of a block called Hattie's Hen House. So who was Hattie? I imagine her as a sweet, elderly aunt who lived on a farm with a beautiful garden full of flowers in all the colours of the rainbow, some of which may have looked like the flower in the block. To emphasise the sense of times gone by I used reproduction fabrics which might well have been used in Hattie's time!

List of materials
Fabric for the blocks
- 36 light and 36 dark 2½in squares for the four-patch blocks
- About 20in of fabric for the border round the four-patch blocks. Choose a fabric which is not too thick and stiff.

Fabric for side and corner triangles, sashings and border
- About 20in of fabric for side and corner triangles around the blocks
- About 6in of fabric for the centre strip of the sashing
- About 10in of fabric for the outer strips of the sashing
- About 27½in of fabric for the border

About 10in of fabric for the binding
Fabric for backing
Cotton batting
Spray adhesive
Glue stick
About 12in of freezer paper

Cutting and assembly instructions Hattie's block
The template for the block is on page 112. Cut and sew 18 blocks.

1 Cutting the Hattie's block
- Cut 2 light and 2 dark pieces, 2½in square, for the four-patch blocks (a) and (b).
- Cut 1 piece, 5½in square, for the fabric round the block (c).

2 Assembly
- Using two (a) and two (b) squares, sew a four-patch block, see page 7. Iron the seams flat.
- Follow the instructions for 'Reverse appliqué by machine' on page 10 to make up Hattie's block. In this case the four-patch block corresponds to the circle in the centre.
- Before you sew the block together, cut into the seam allowance, as indicated by the circles in the diagram opposite,

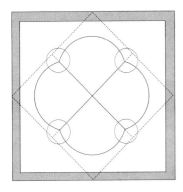

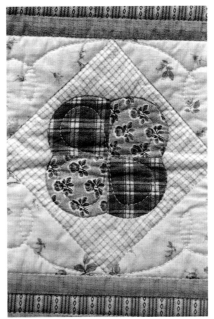

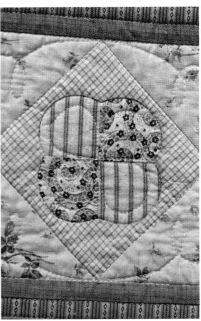

At a distance the background fabric in the blocks merges with the side triangles to form light coloured stripes in the quilt.

through all layers of fabric and to within 2-3 threads of the line. This makes it easier to sew right into the corner.

• Sew 18 blocks and trim to 5in square.

Side and corner triangles

1 Cutting

• 8 pieces, 8in square, cut diagonally to make 32 side triangles (d) of which 30 are needed. Note: if the fabric has a one-way pattern you must take this into account when cutting.
• 6 pieces, 4½in square, cut diagonally to make 12 triangles (e).
• 4 strips, 1 × 38½in, to form the centre strip of the sashing.
• 8 strips, 1 × 38½in, to form the outer strips of the sashing.

2 Assembly

• Sew two side triangles (d) to each side of a block, as shown in the diagram.
• Corner triangles (e) are attached at the top and bottom of each row of blocks.
• Sew three strips like this.
• Trim the rows of blocks to 6⅞ × 38½in.
• To make a strip set sashing sew together: an outer strip, centre strip and outer strip.
• Repeat until you have four strip sets.
• Trim the strip sets to 2 × 38½in.
• Sew together the strip sets and block strips.
• Trim to 25⅞ × 38½in.

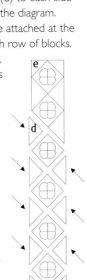

Outer border

1 Cutting

• 2 pieces, 5½ × 38½in, of the border fabric (f).
• 2 pieces, 5½ × 35½in, of the border fabric (g).

2 Assembly

• Sew the two borders (f) to the sides of the quilt.
• Sew the two borders (g) to the top and bottom of the quilt.
• Trim to 35⅞ × 48½in. (You could leave the trimming until after you have finished the quilting and you are ready to attach the binding.)

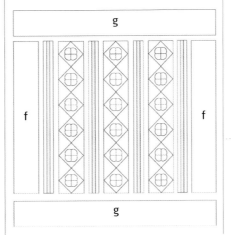

Quilting

The quilt is machine quilted with silk thread using stitch in the ditch, along the seams including the one between the four-patch block and background in the Hattie's Hen House blocks. A stylized flower is quilted on each four-patch block. A quilt pattern is drawn in the border using a plastic template and marking chalk.

Binding

For the binding you need a strip 150in long. The method is described in Techniques on pages 14 and 15.

Dressed for the Party

DESIGNED BY: Rie Norum
HAND QUILTED BY: Rie Norum
TABLECLOTH DIMENSIONS: 24 × 42½in
FINISHED BLOCK SIZE: 4½in square

If you want to learn reverse appliqué on a sewing machine, this is the block to start with! It uses only two parts and has been my sample block when I have held courses in this technique. Every time I have demonstrated how to sew it I have ended up with a new block, and eventually all these blocks were used to make this little party tablecloth. The sequin ribbon edging makes it really special. Pearls and sequins were added to create a gentle transition to the sequin ribbons.

List of materials
Fabric for the blocks
- 10 pieces, 5½in square, for the block backgrounds
- 10 pieces, 4in square, for the circles

Fabric for sashing, insertions and border
- About 6in of fabric for sashing
- About 14in of fabric for insertions
- About 6in of fabric for the side border
- About 14in of fabric for the outer border

About 10in of fabric for binding
Fabric for backing
Cotton batting
Spray adhesive
Glue stick
About 12in of freezer paper

Cutting and assembly instructions
Circle block
The template for the block is on page 118.
Cut and sew 10 blocks.

1 Cutting a circle block
- Cut 1 piece, 5½in square, of background fabric for the block (a).
- Cut 1 piece, 4in square, for the circle in the centre (b).

2 Assembly
- Sew part (a) and part (b) together as described in 'Reverse appliqué by machine' on page 10 to make a block.
- Make 10 blocks like this.
- Trim the blocks to 5in square.

Sashing and insertions
1 Cutting
- 12 pieces, 2 × 5in, for the insertions (c).
- 3 pieces, 4 × 32in, for the sashing (d).

2 Assembly
- Sew two rows consisting of block (a) + (b) and insertion (c), starting and finishing with (c).
- Sew sashings (d) on each side of the block rows, starting and finishing with (d).

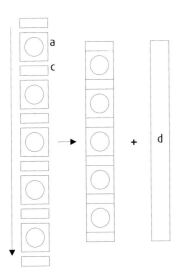

Side border and outer border

1 Cutting

- 2 pieces, 2½ × 32in, of the side border fabric (e).
- 2 pieces, 5¾ × 24in, of the top and bottom border fabric (f).

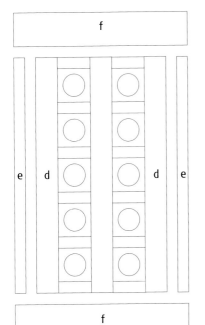

2 Assembly

- Sew the two side edges (e) to the sashings (d) on either side of the cloth.
- Sew the two remaining outer edges (f) to the top and bottom of the cloth.
- Trim to 24 × 42½in. (You could leave the trimming until you have finished quilting and are ready to attach the binding.)

The tablecloth is hand quilted using silk thread. You will find the pattern for the quilting within the circle at the back of the book. The pattern is transferred to the fabric using tulle.

Quilting

The quilt is hand quilted with silk thread using stitch in the ditch for all the seams including those within the blocks. The template for the quilting pattern inside the block is on page 118. The quilting pattern on the sashing (d) was first drawn on tulle and then transferred on to the fabric (see Equipment, page 5). The quilt pattern on the wide outer borders (f) was drawn using a plastic template and marking chalk.

Sequin ribbon

The sequin ribbon is optional. Pin it to the wide outer borders, tack (baste) in place and sew on by hand. Trim the ribbon along the outer edges of the tablecloth and remove any sequins which will cause problems when sewing on the binding.

Binding

For the binding you need a strip 125in long. The method is described in Techniques on pages 14 and 15.

Flowers for Abelone

DESIGNED BY: Rie Norum
MACHINE QUILTED BY: Rie Norum
FINISHED QUILT SIZE: 41 × 55in
FINISHED BLOCK SIZE: Square: 7½in square. Flower: 3⅛in diameter

When your eyesight is not so good, it is important to have plenty of contrast if you are to find your way around. This is the case for my daughter, Abelone, so I wanted to give her a whole flower garden she could touch and feel and with lots of contrasting colours. After a number of attempts I came up with a flower I could sew by machine. The background consists of light shirting fabrics, while the rest of the fabrics are reproductions.

The flower is a stylized version of the 'Harrison Rose', which originated in the American state of Indiana in the 1860s. The stems of the flowers were made using a bias tape maker and iron-on interfacing tape. The flowers and stems are appliquéd by hand.

List of materials

Fabric for backgrounds and stems
- 24 pieces, 7½in square, of various shirting fabrics
- About 16in of green fabric

Fabric for flowers
- About 12in red fabric
- About 10 × 20in yellow fabric
- About 10 × 12in pink fabric

Fabric for the border
- Inner border: 10in or 48in if you prefer not to cut and join
- Outer border: 32in or 48in if you prefer not to cut and join

About 12in of fabric for binding
Fabric for backing
Cotton batting
Spray adhesive
Glue stick
About 12in of freezer paper
A ½in fusible bias tape maker and ⅜in fusible interfacing to make the flower stems.
Plastic template sheet for positioning the flower stems.

Cutting and assembly instructions
Central section
1 **Cutting the blocks**
- 24 squares, 7½in square, for background (a). In this quilt I used 24 different light shirting fabrics.

2 **Assembling the central section**
- Spread the squares out and sew them together in rows of four, making six rows.

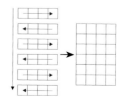

- Sew the six rows together. Iron the seam allowances in alternate directions before you sew the rows together, as shown in the diagram.

Inner border

1 Cutting

- 2 pieces, 1½ × 42½in, of inner border fabric (b).
- 2 pieces, 1½ × 30½in, of inner border fabric (c).

2 Assembly

- Sew the two border pieces (b) to the sides of the quilt.
- Sew the two border pieces (c) to the top and bottom of the quilt.

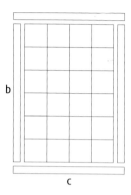

Outer border

1 Cutting

- 2 pieces, 5¾ × 44½in, of outer border fabric (d).
- 2 pieces, 5¾ × 41in, of outer border fabric (e).

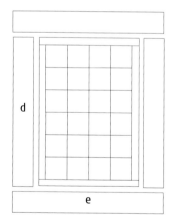

2 Assembly

- Sew the two outer borders (d) to the sides of the quilt.
- Sew the two outer borders (e) to the top and bottom of the quilt.
- Trim to 41 × 55in. (You could leave the trimming until you have finished quilting and are ready to attach the binding.)
- The quilt is now ready for the addition of the roses and stems.

Flower stems

1 Cutting

24 strips, 1 × 15in, of the flower stem fabric. Cut the fabric on the bias, that is, at 45 degrees to the weave of the fabric.

2 Preparing the flower stems

- I used a couple of handy products which enabled me to make the flower stems very quickly. These were a ½in fusible bias tape maker and ⅜in fusible interfacing, see page 6.
- Pull the fabric and adhesive tape through the bias tape maker while ironing the tape in place. (See the instructions given with the bias tape maker.)
- If you don't have a bias tape maker, you can make bias tape by folding in a seam allowance along each edge of the strip and ironing, taking care to keep the width constant.
- Make 24 strips.

Sewing on

- Pin the stems to the quilt top making S-shapes, as shown in the diagram. To shape and position the stems right, make the plastic template given on page 119.
- Trim the ends so that there is no overlap.
- Iron to fix the adhesive before you remove the pins.
- Now sew the stems in place by hand, using invisible stitching or quilt stitch. If you choose to sew the stems by machine there are many options, including quilt stitch, invisible machine appliqué or fine zigzag stitch.

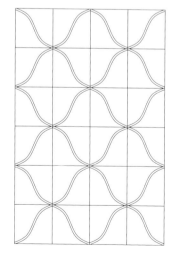

Roses

The template for the rose is on page 118.

1 Cutting

- 18 pieces, 1½in square, of fabric for the centre of the flower (f).
- 144 pieces, ¾ × 1½in, of fabric for the small petals (g).
- 144 pieces, 1½ × 1½in, of fabric for the large petals (h).

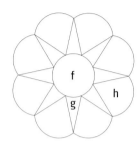

2 Assembly

- Sew the roses using parts (f), (g) and (h). This can be done simply and accurately using the technique 'Piecing using freezer paper' on page 11.
- Draw the block on freezer paper. Cut out the central part (f) of the block and then fold along all the lines.

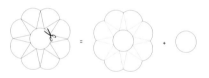

- Iron the freezer paper with the glossy side against the wrong side of fabric square (g).
- Fold back the freezer paper, place square (h) on square (g), right sides facing, and sew along the edge of the paper, taking care not to sew through the paper. Fold the fabric against the glossy side of the freezer paper and iron flat from the wrong side. Continue all the way round. When you have sewn together all the parts and only have the last seam to do, mark where the seam is to be on the back of the last two pieces.
- Peel the work from each side of the freezer paper, place the parts right sides facing, pin and sew them together. Iron the freezer paper again.
- Iron the flower centre part which you cut out of the freezer paper flower block on to fabric square (f). Cut out, adding a seam allowance of ¼in from the edge.

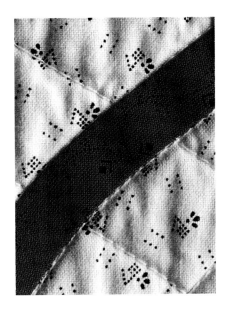

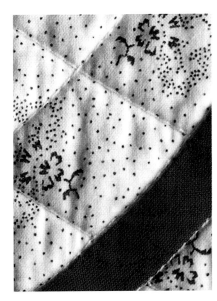

- Tack (baste) around the seam allowance and pull tight so that the seam allowance folds in towards the freezer paper. Make sure you have a nice, neat edge and tie off the thread. Place the flower centre in the centre of the flower and sew in place with invisible stitching.
- Sew a total of 18 roses.

viewed from the wrong side

3 Sewing on the roses

- Trim round the outside of the freezer paper at least ¼in from the edge and cut slits in the fabric about ¼in apart. The slits should not be cut closer than 2–3 threads from the line and the edge of the freezer paper.
- Spray adhesive along the cut edge of the fabric. To avoid spraying on the freezer paper, draw the block on ordinary paper, and fix it to the front of the block, covering the freezer paper exactly while you spray with the adhesive. Fold the fabric against the freezer paper and the wrong side of the fabric. Alternatively you can tack (baste) the edge of the freezer paper in place.
- Iron the block from the wrong side so that the edge lifts off the freezer paper. Remove the freezer paper and fold down the edge again. Apply adhesive using a glue stick along the edge of the fabric.
- Place a rose on the quilt at the intersection of two stems, as shown in the diagram. Using an iron on the wrong side, press lightly around the edge to fix the adhesive. You can also baste the rose in place by hand instead of using adhesive.
- Now sew all the roses in place by hand, using invisible stitching or quilt stitch. If you choose to sew the roses by machine there are many options, including invisible machine appliqué, quilt stitch or fine zigzag.

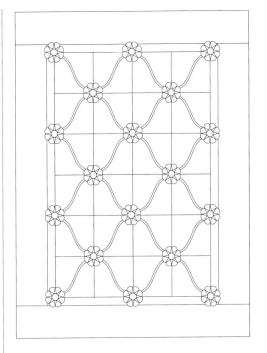

Quilting

The quilt is machine quilted with silk thread using stitch in the ditch on all seams including those round the flower and the flower centre. The areas between the flower stems are quilted with a criss-cross pattern with the help of an edge ruler, which is fitted to the pressure foot rod and helps keep a constant distance between the quilt seams. A leaf pattern is used for the outer frame.

Binding

For the binding you need a strip 205in long. The method is described in Techniques on pages 14 and 15.

Wheels on the Bus

DESIGNED BY: Rie Norum
MACHINE QUILTED BY: Rie Norum
FINISHED QUILT SIZE: 38 × 47½in
FINISHED BLOCK SIZE: Pinwheel block, 6in square

With small children you hear a lot of children's songs, some of which become favourites. I have caught myself humming 'The wheels on the bus go round and round' while sewing, long after the kids are in bed. This quilt got its name from the block inside the circle which is called a pinwheel. The background fabrics of the blocks are woven with different coloured threads in the warp and weft. which gives them more life than a fabric which is dyed one colour. The plain fabric sashing and filler pieces emphasise the blocks. The border is a beautiful Japanese floral fabric.

List of materials

Fabric for the pinwheel blocks

- Various fabrics for backgrounds, 6½in square
- Various fabrics for pinwheels

Fabric for sashing, corner stones, side and corner triangles and outer border

- About 16in of fabric for sashing
- About 8in of fabric for the corner stones in the sashing
- About 12in of fabric for side and corner triangles
- About 24in of fabric for the outer border

About 8in of fabric for binding
Fabric for backing
Cotton batting
Spray adhesive
Glue stick
About 12in of freezer paper

Cutting and assembly instructions
Pinwheel block

The template for the block is on page 117.
Cut and sew 18 blocks.

1 Cutting

- Cut two 2¼ × 4½in rectangles in light fabric (a) and cut each diagonally at 45 degrees (see diagram below) to give two triangles, four in all. Cut two rectangles in dark fabric (b) in the same way to give four triangles. (The whole quilt uses 72 light and 72 dark triangles.)
- 1 piece, 6½in square, of background fabric (c).

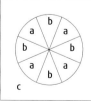

2 Assembly

- Using the eight (a) and (b) triangles, sew the pinwheel blocks. The pinwheel itself inside the circle can be sewn simply and accurately using the technique Piecing using freezer paper on page 11. Use the template on page 117 to draw the block on freezer paper, including the dotted lines outside the circle. These are used to position the pinwheel circle before gluing the block in place. Cut out the central part of the block and then fold along all the lines. Cut the circle in two along one of the lines. The two halves are sewn separately.

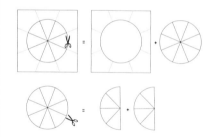

- Iron freezer paper, with the glossy side against the wrong side of the fabric, on one of the triangles (a) or (b), as shown in the diagram below. Make sure that you start each half with the same fabric.

 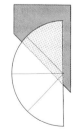

- Fold the freezer paper back, place a new triangle with its right side against the first part and sew along the edge of the paper. Be careful not to sew through the paper! Fold the fabric against the freezer paper and iron flat.

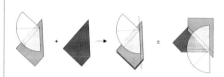

- Continue until both semicircles are complete. Trim them (¼in) along the straight edge, pin the halves together exactly and sew along the edge of the paper without sewing through it. The seams will now be folded against the matt side of the freezer paper. Iron the seams apart.

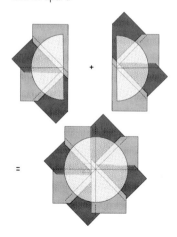

- Leave the pinwheel while you complete the outer edge (c) of the block.

- Iron freezer paper, with the glossy side against the wrong side of the fabric, on (c) and follow the description for Reverse appliqué by machine on page 10. Make sure the edge of the paper runs along the weave of the fabric. When you glue the block in place, the dotted guide lines you drew on (c) should coincide with the seams on the pinwheel block.

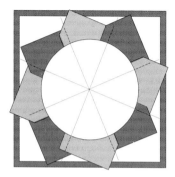

- Sew 18 blocks like this.
- Trim the blocks to 6in square.

Sashing, corner stones, side and corner triangles and filler pieces

1 Cutting
- 48 pieces, 1¾ × 6in, for sashing (d).
- 17 pieces, 1¾in square, for corner stones (e).
- 7 pieces, 2¼in square, cut diagonally to make 14 corner triangles for the sashing ends (f).
- 3 pieces, 9in square cut diagonally to make 12 side triangles (g) of which 10 are needed. Note: If the fabric has a one way pattern, you must take this into account when cutting.
- 2 pieces, 4¾in square, cut diagonally to make 4 corner triangles (h).

2 Assembly
- Sew blocks (c) and (d) together in rows diagonally starting and and finishing with a side triangle (g) as shown in the diagram.
- Sew sashings (d) and (e) together in rows diagonally starting and finishing with triangle (f).
- Sew together the diagonal rows of blocks and sashings.
- Finish by sewing triangle (h) in the four corners.
- Trim the central section.

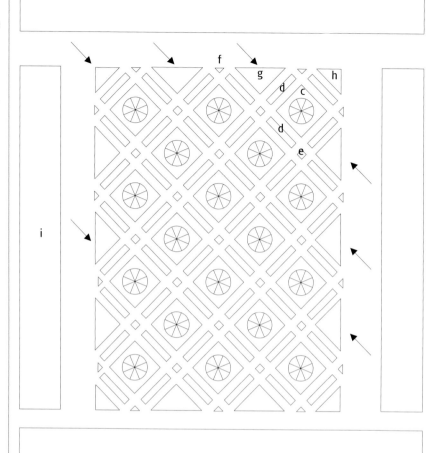

Outer border

1 Cutting
- 4 pieces, 5¼ × 38in, of the outer border fabric (i).

2 Assembly
- Sew two outer borders (i) to the sides of the quilt.
- Sew the two remaining outer borders (i) to the top and bottom of the quilt.
- Trim to 38 × 47½in. (You could leave the trimming until you have finished quilting and are ready to attach the binding.)

Quilting

The quilt is hand quilted using stitch in the ditch and silk thread. A spiral is quilted inside the blocks, see page 117 for the pattern. A row of stitching is quilted round the pinwheel circle, ¼in from the edge. Two rows of stitching are quilted, 3/8in from each edge of the sashing, in both directions. The side triangles have three lines quilted from the point of the triangle, evenly spaced along the outer border. The corner triangles, are quilted in the same way from the point of the triangle. A wide pattern is used for the outer border.

Binding

For the binding you need a strip 185in long. The method is described in Techniques on pages 14 and 15.

Suppliers

You can find patchwork supplies in good haberdashery and fabric departments of large stores. For more specialist materials such as batting, templates, quilt patterns, etc there are craft shops which specialise in patchwork and quilting. Otherwise on line suppliers offer an excellent service.

UK

The Cotton Patch
1283–1285 Stratford Road
Hall Green
Birmingham B28 9AJ

Tel: 0121 702 2840
www.cottonpatch.co.uk

Fireside Fabrics
Unit 26 Zan Industrial Park
Crewe Road
Wheelock,
Sandbach
Cheshire CW11 4QH

www.firesidefabrics.co.uk

www.houseofpatchwork.co.uk

Lady Sew and Sew
Moy House
57 Institute Road
Marlow
Bucks SL7 1BN

Tel: 01628 890532
www.ladysewandsew.co.uk

Pauline's Patchwork
Brewers Quay, Hope Square
Weymouth
Dorset DT4 8TR

Tel: 01305 766543
www.paulinespatchwork.co.uk

Pelenna Patchworks
5 Bevans Terrace
Pontrhydyfen
Port Talbot SA12 9TR

Tel: 01639 898444
www.pelennapatchworks.co.uk

The Quilt Room
Rear Carvilles, Station Road
Dorking RH4 1XH

Tel: 01306 877307
www.quiltroom.co.uk

Quilt Studio
Unit 26 Zan Industrial Park
Crewe Road
Wheelock, Sandbach
Cheshire CW11 4QH,

Tel: 0870 300 1692
www.quiltstudio.co.uk

The Tabbycat Ltd
Muffin Corner
29 Church Street
Brigg DN20 0RG

Tel:01652-680776
www.thetabbycat.co.uk

www.craft-fair.co.uk

USA

Websites which list on-line patchwork and quilting suppliers throughout the USA:

www.fabshophop.com

www.fabric.com

The following sites are also worth visiting:

www.fatquarterquilters.com

www.lovingfabrics.com

www.planetpatchwork.com

www.virginiaquilter.com

Patterns

Green Tweed Handbag
Page 92

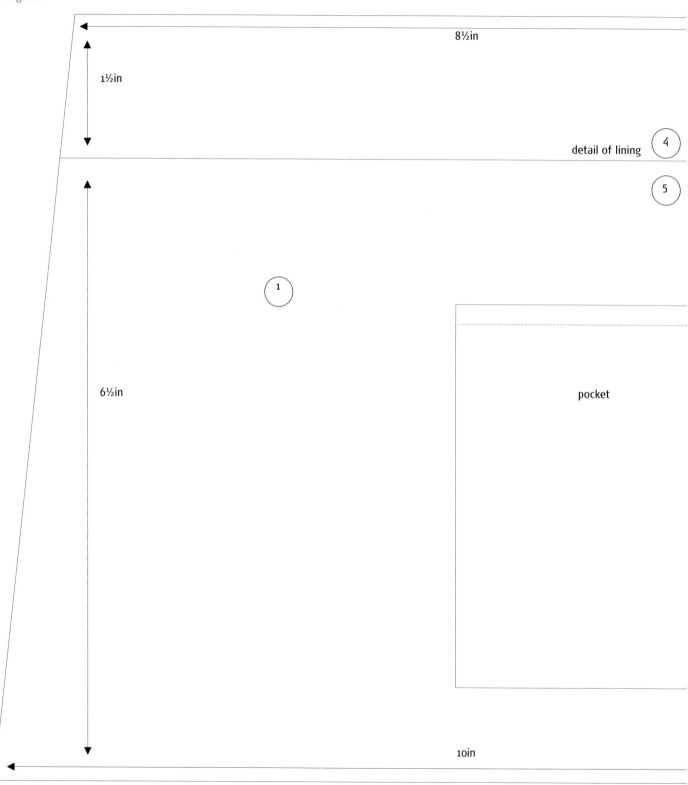

8½in

1½in

detail of lining 4

5

1

6½in

pocket

10in

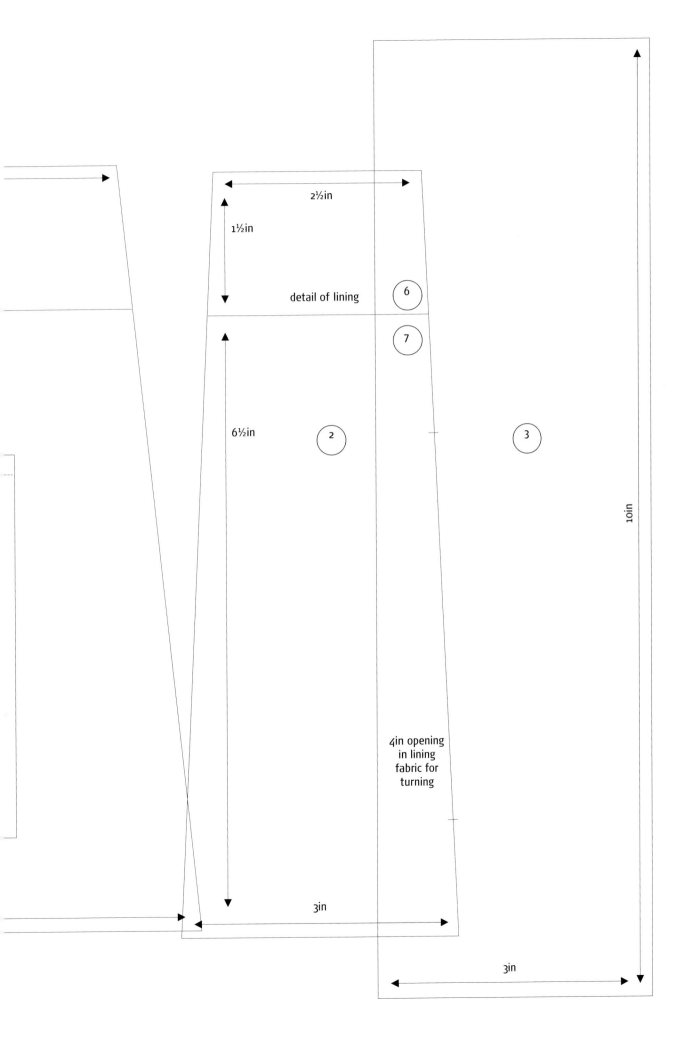

2½in

1½in

detail of lining 6

7

6½in 2 3

10in

4in opening
in lining
fabric for
turning

3in

3in

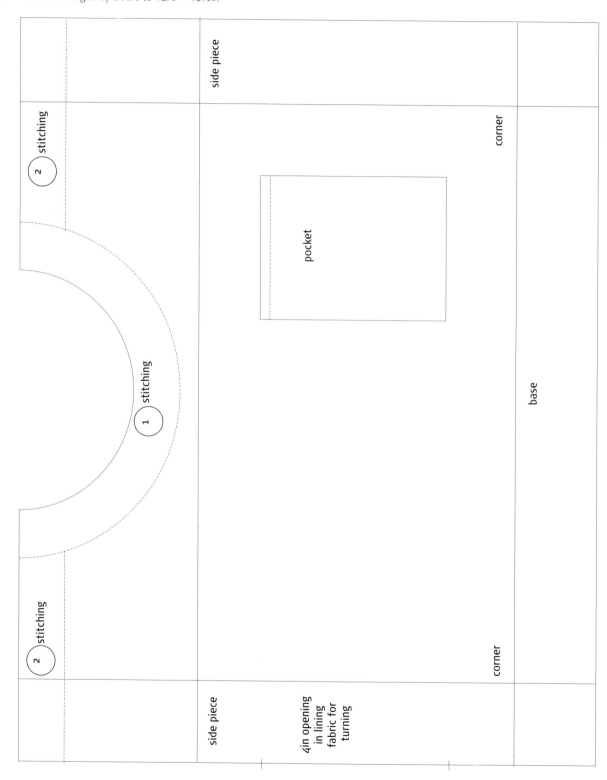

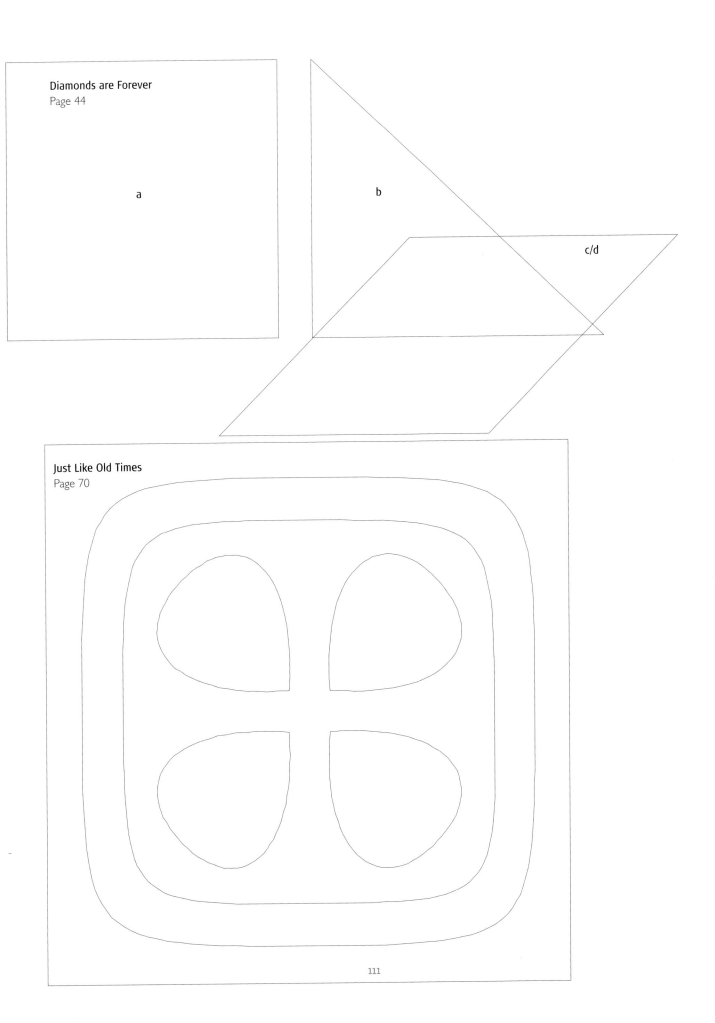

Diamonds are Forever
Page 44

a

b

c/d

Just Like Old Times
Page 70

Dear Hattie
Page 96

Star Boat and Star Boat tablecloth
Pages 58 and 62

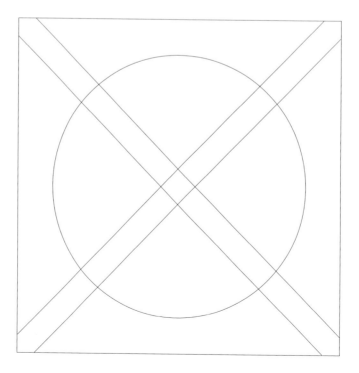

Star Boat
Page 58
The pattern should be enlarged by 200% to 12in square

the parts are drawn in reverse

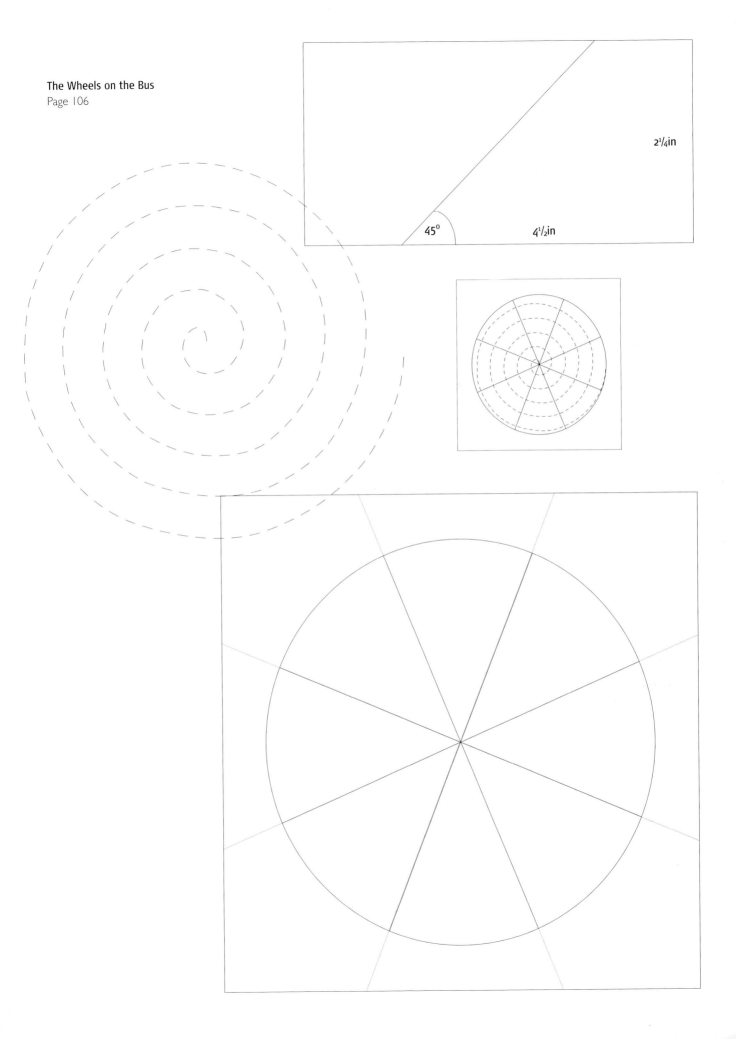

A Page to colour...
Pages 86-89

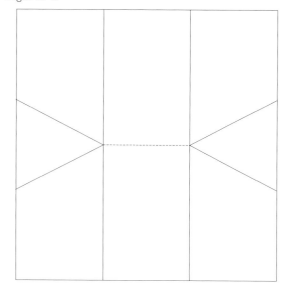

Flowers for Abelone
Page 100

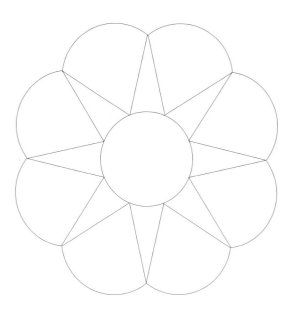

Dressed for the Party
Page 98

Postscript

*We have been lucky to have so many people helping us. We'd like to
thank them all, first and foremost:*

The Norum, Morkemo and Krohg families
Patient husbands and grandparents for babysitting and encouragement
along the way. We'd especially like to thank Rie's mother, Margrethe,
who is so versatile! She has made many trips by air from Bodø in
northern Norway down to Oslo where we live. She has helped us
with the children, kept us well fed and last but not least contributed
some meticulous sewing. Margrethe is the epitome of exactness, and
has taught us a lot that we didn't know!

Cappelen
Thanks to Karin Mundal for believing in our quilts and styles. Creativity
is a source of excitement, and it is tempting to do everything at once
when one is creating a book! That's when it is good to have somebody
there to make sure we keep our feet on the ground and to ensure
consistency. Thanks to stylist Ingrid Skaansar and photographer Grethe
Syvertsen Arnstad. You have presented our work brilliantly, in attractive
surroundings. You have managed to show off our quilts from their best
side. The locations you chose were perfect: to think our quilts have
even been to Skagen in Denmark!

Husqvarna Viking
Thank you very much for close co-operation and your excellent
sewing machines. In our opinion, Husqvarna Viking Designer SE is the
world's best sewing machine!

Our local quilting milieu
Thanks to Kathrine's Quiltestue og Lappe Makeriet for greeting us
with a smiling face and some words of encouragement and for all the
beautiful fabrics you have in your shops. These are an endless source
of inspiration. A special thank you to Trine Bakke, who has inspired us
to see fabrics and colours in new ways. Thanks to the members of
our sewing club, who helped us on the home straight with cries of
encouragement and by sewing on hanging channels. Thank you to Unni
Gullvåg for the use of her pattern for the princess bags. And last, but
not least, a huge thank you to Anne Fjellvær, our sewing club friend,
who took pity on us in the final stages of the book project and helped
us with hand quilting, machine quilting and sewing on binding. Without
you, Anne, we would never have met our deadlines. Many thanks to
you also for your great quilting tips!

Hilde to Rie and Rie to Hilde
Maybe we have slightly different styles. At least, we did before we
started writing a book together. Rie sews in series, in other words, first
comes design, then sewing, assembly and finishing with neatly attached
binding. Then on to the next project. Hilde sews in parallel – prefers
starting things to finishing things and works with lots of projects at the
same time, in many different phases. Rie is accurate, and on her quilts
all the corners meet. Hilde is a bit more haphazard and accepts some
lumps and accidents.

At least, that's the way it was, but now we have learnt from each
other. Rie's techniques simplify matters, and have helped Hilde to avoid
shortcuts. Rie now has lots of projects under way simultaneously and
has come to like that!

plastic template for flower stems